THE
ERNST & YOUNG
GUIDE TO TAKING YOUR
COMPANY PUBLIC

Also from Ernst & Young LLP

The Ernst & Young Business Plan Guide, Second Edition
The Ernst & Young Guide to Financing for Growth
Ernst & Young's Personal Financial Planning Guide
The Ernst & Young Tax Guide
The Ernst & Young Tax-Saving Strategies Guide
The Name of the Game: The Business of Sports
Managing Information Strategically: Increase Your Company's Competitiveness and Efficiency by Using Information as a Strategic Tool
Development Effectiveness: Strategies for IS Organizational Transition
Privatization: Investing in State-Owned Enterprises Around the World
The Ernst & Young Almanac and Guide to U.S. Business Cities: 65 Leading Places to Do Business
The Ernst & Young Guide to Total Cost Management
The Complete Guide to Special Event Management
Mergers and Acquisitions, Second Edition
Understanding and Using Financial Data: An Ernst & Young Guide for Attorneys

Forthcoming from Ernst & Young LLP

Information Management for Healthcare Organizations
Strategies for Accelerating the Information Systems Delivery Process After Reengineering

The
Ernst & Young
Guide to Taking Your
Company Public

Stephen C. Blowers
Gregory K. Ericksen
Thomas L. Milan

John Wiley & Sons, Inc.
New York • Chichester • Brisbane • Toronto • Singapore

Copyright © 1995 by Ernst & Young
Published by John Wiley & Sons, Inc.

Library of Congress Cataloging in Publication Data:

Blowers, Stephen C.
    The Ernst & Young guide to taking your company public / Stephen C.
Blowers, Gregory K. Ericksen, Thomas L. Milan.
      p.   cm.
    Includes bibliographical references.
    ISBN 0-471-11473-1 (cloth : alk. paper). — ISBN 0-471-11474-X
(pbk. : alk. paper)
      1. Going public (Securities)   2. Corporations—Finance.
3. Private companies—Finance.   I. Ericksen, Gregory.   II. Milan,
Thomas L.   III. Title.   IV. Title: Guide to taking your company public.
HG4028.S7B553   1995
658.15′224—dc20   94-40296

CONTENTS

PREFACE

Why do you want to go public? Is it the opportunity to expand your company? The prestige of being listed on a stock exchange? Providing a means for you and key employees to cash in on the company you have grown and nurtured with your vision, persistence, and hard work? Sounds good? But are you familiar with the registration process and underwriting agreements, the SEC's ongoing requirements, dealing with securities analysts and demanding shareholders?

This book has been written to provide owners and executives of privately held businesses with a comprehensive, up-to-date reference to assist in evaluating the complex elements and consequences of going public. It will show you what to expect from the SEC, financial community, press, and shareholders. You will learn the details of the "going public" process and how to successfully work with attorneys, underwriters, and auditors.

Going public may not be the best choice for you or your company. It might be a good idea, but to maximize the value of your offering perhaps you should wait 12 to 24 months to restructure your operations. How do you know what decision is best? Alternatives to going public also are discussed in this work.

If you are thinking about going public, this book will help you decide if that is the right alternative for your growing company.

STEPHEN C. BLOWERS
GREGORY K. ERICKSEN
THOMAS L. MILAN

ACKNOWLEDGMENTS

The scope of experience reflected in this book is the result of contributions from many professionals at Ernst & Young LLP. As accountants and consultants of Ernst & Young's Entrepreneurial Services practice, we advise and help emerging and medium-size companies select and gain the means of financing, including taking their companies public. We have learned from our vast experience that few business activities have a more profound effect on the company's owners and its management than taking your company public. All of us thought we could make an especially meaningful contribution by sharing our knowledge in this area with growing businesses.

The Ernst & Young contributors are:

Gerald B. Wilson	Atlanta
Dennis R. Baltzley	Boston
Thomas D. Vogelsinger	Chicago
James A. Hassett	Cincinnati
Herbert S. Braun	Cleveland
Edward B. Beanland	Dallas
Kevin M. Smith	Denver
Bryan A. Becker	Detroit
Ronald P. Pettirossi	Hartford
Lawrence D. Rodriguez	Honolulu
Daniel R. Reese	Houston
Jay W. Heck	Indianapolis
Kurt H. Mueller	Kansas City
Mark C. Nelson	Los Angeles

Bernard Leone	MetroPark
Dan L. Andersen	Milwaukee
Darryl L. Thorvilson	Minneapolis
Laurence N. Charney	New York
N. Robert Kopecko	Norfolk
Richard D. Corn	Oklahoma City
Stephen J. Negrotti	Philadelphia
Adam S. Monks	Pittsburgh
David W. Jessen	Raleigh
Don N. Ecker	Riverside
A. P. Jennings	San Antonio
James Pangburn	San Jose
Rodolfo A. Colberg	San Juan
Richard P. Fox	Seattle
Leyton B. Broughton	St. Louis
Richard Dobkin	Tampa
William H. Washecka	Washington, D.C.

Other important contributions were made by a number of Ernst & Young professionals, including Patrick F. Minan, Washington, D.C.; Carlo D. Pippolo, Washington, D.C.; Ronald L. McCrummen, St. Louis; David A. Farrell, Washington, D.C.; Joseph A. King, New York; John F. McCarthy, Boston; John E. Moyer, Atlanta; and Michael Moneymaker, Richmond.

Special thanks also go to Dr. Larry Singleton, Ph.D., George Washington University who provided invaluable help in drafting the appendices on *Board of Directors* and *Accounting and Reporting Issues Associated with Initial Public Offering*, and to John T. Wall, Executive Vice President at The Nasdaq Stock Market, for providing the material in Appendix A.

Finally, we thank Mort Meyerson, Ernst & Young's director of public communications, who first suggested this book, and then helped plan and develop it.

1

WHAT IT MEANS TO BECOME A PUBLIC COMPANY

The siren song of the public market can be strong indeed. Every year, hundreds of companies are drawn to that market by its many significant benefits. Guided by experienced, aggressive management teams and supported by a strong cast of professional advisors, many of these companies take their new capital and parlay it into unprecedented growth.

But going public is not a panacea. The fairy-tale success stories are counterbalanced by many tales of plunging share prices accompanied by litigation conflicts, management shakeouts, and loss of control. Some of these companies would have failed anyway, but others could have avoided disaster. Management may be daunted by the dimensions and rigors of managing a public company. Poor market timing and lack of adequate planning and preparation also can jeopardize the initial public offering.

In short, going public can provide many benefits and opportunities, but the cost can be substantial. This chapter will review the benefits and drawbacks as well as the continuing obligations involved in going public. The considerations discussed here relate mainly to going public with a share offering, but many are equally applicable to initial public offerings of debt securities.

BENEFITS AND OPPORTUNITIES

The benefits of going public are many and diverse. To determine whether they outweigh the drawbacks, you must evaluate them in the context of both shareholder and corporate objectives. Some of the most attractive benefits include:

- **Improved Financial Condition.** The sale by the company of shares to the public brings money that does not have to be repaid, immediately improving the company's financial condition.

- **Greater Marketability.** Once a company goes public, the owners often find themselves in a new and more favorable position. Instead of holding shares with limited marketability, they will hold shares that can easily be sold in the market (subject to certain restrictions if their shares are unregistered) or used as collateral for loans.

- **Improved Value.** The value of the stock may increase remarkably, starting with the initial offering. Shares that are publicly traded generally command higher prices than those that are not. There are at least three reasons why investors are usually willing to pay more for public companies: (1) the marketability of the shares, (2) the maturity/sophistication attributed to public companies, and (3) the availability of more information.

- **Diversification of Personal Portfolios.** Going public makes it possible for shareholders to diversify their investment portfolios. Initial public offerings often include a secondary offering (shares owned by existing shareholders) in addition to a primary offering (previously unissued shares). You must ensure that potential investors and shareholders do not perceive the secondary offering as a bailout for existing shareholders. Underwriters frequently restrict the number of shares that can be sold by existing shareholders in a secondary offering.

    Before you opt for diversification, you need to decide whether it is an appropriate goal. Spreading investment risk in this way may be as relevant an objective for the shareholders of a private company as it is for an institutional investor. However, many private companies earn returns well in excess of normal investment returns. You need to consider your company's prospects, the degree of inherent risk in your industry, and the return your company's shareholders earn now compared with what they could earn in alternative investments. Diversification may be a good idea, but this is not always the case.

- **Estate Planning.** Going public also helps with estate planning because the liquidity of a shareholder's estate is increased by the sale of shares. Having an existing public market for shares retained also makes it easier for the company to hold future secondary offerings of shares. Should that future secondary offering be precipitated by the death of a major shareholder who is a key member of the management team, however, the offering may not be well received by investors.

  The taxable value of a deceased investor's estate can be determined more easily if the shares owned are publicly traded. The value of those shares, moreover, will often be increased by a public market. Executors may be forced to sell a private company to pay estate taxes, whereas they can sell only a portion of the shares in a public company to pay them. Many of the estate tax benefits available to a privately held company also will apply once your company is public.

- **Capital to Sustain Growth.** The net proceeds from the sale of shares in a public offering provide working capital for the company—an obvious benefit. The company can use this capital for general corporate purposes or apply it to more specific projects. For example, it can use the capital to acquire other businesses, repay debt, finance research and development projects, and acquire or modernize production facilities. Another plus is that raising equity capital through a public offering often results in a higher valuation for your company, through a higher multiple of earnings (or price-earnings ratio), as compared with many types of private

financing. Thus, it often results in less dilution of ownership than with some other financing alternatives, such as
venture capital. Raising capital in this way also avoids the
interest costs and cash drain of debt financing.

- **Improved Opportunities for Future Financing.** By going
public, a company usually improves its net worth and builds
a larger and broader equity base. The improved debt-to-
equity ratio will help you borrow additional funds as
needed or reduce your current cost of borrowing. If your
stock performs well in the continuing aftermarket, you will
be able to raise additional equity capital on favorable terms.
With an established market for your stock, you will have
the flexibility to offer future investors a whole new range of
securities with liquidity and an ascertainable market value.

- **A Path to Mergers and Acquisitions.** Private companies
often lack the financial connections and resources to assume an aggressive role in mergers and acquisitions. Well-
conceived acquisitions can play a big part in corporate
survival and success. A merger can be the route to instant
product diversification and quick completion of product
lines. It also can provide technical know-how, greater executive depth, economies of scale, improved access to financing, entry into otherwise closed markets, vertical
integration of manufacturing operations, and new marketing strength. Going public enhances a company's financing alternatives for acquisitions by adding two vital
components to its financial resources: cash derived from
the initial offering and un-issued equity shares that have
a ready market.

  Public companies often issue stock (instead of paying
cash) to acquire other businesses. Owners of a company
you seek to acquire may be more willing to accept your
company's stock if it is publicly traded. The liquidity provided by the public market affords them greater flexibility—they can more easily sell their shares when it suits
their needs, or use the shares as collateral for loans.

The public market also assists in valuing the company's shares. If your shares are privately held, you have to estimate their value and hope the owners of the other company will agree; if they don't, you will have to negotiate a "fair price." On the other hand, if the shares are publicly traded, the price per share generally is set every day in the stock market where the shares are traded.

- **Enhanced Corporate Image and Increased Employee Participation.** Having a public market for its securities can improve your company's corporate image and indirectly strengthen its competitive position. The attention of the financial community and press is focused on your company as it goes public, so you receive free publicity and word-of-mouth advertising from investors, boosting your corporate image. In addition, some of your customers and suppliers may purchase shares in your initial public offering, which may lead to new loyalties.

  Once you have established a public market for your shares, you may be better able to attract and retain key employees by offering them stock options, stock purchase plans, and stock appreciation rights. These popular compensation arrangements not only conserve cash and offer tax advantages, but also increase employee motivation and loyalty.

- **Listing on a Stock Exchange.** A goal of many companies that go public is to be listed on a stock exchange. A listing facilitates trading in your company's stock and fosters public recognition because listed companies are generally more closely watched by the financial press.

  The listing requirements set by the various exchanges differ. Some companies can meet the requirements of the New York Stock Exchange on an initial public offering. Others are better suited to the American and the regional stock exchanges who generally have less restrictive listing requirements. An increasing number of new public companies that could qualify for stock exchange listing choose to have their shares traded on the over-the-counter market. An expanded discussion of choosing between exchange listing versus over-the-counter trading is included in Chapter 6 and Appendix A.

DRAWBACKS AND CONTINUING OBLIGATIONS

Now let us consider some disadvantages of going public. Here again, you must view the possible drawbacks in the context of your company's objectives. In many cases, you can minimize the impact of these disadvantages through thoughtful planning backed by the help of outside advisors.

- **Loss of Control.** Depending on the proportion of shares sold to the public, you may be at risk of losing control of your company now or in the future. Retaining at least 51 percent of the shares will ensure control for now, but subsequent offerings and acquisitions may dilute your control. A wide distribution of your shares will ensure that there is no concentration of voting power in a few hands, reducing the immediate threat to your control. Nevertheless, you may still be susceptible to an unfriendly takeover.

  However, if the stock is widely distributed, management usually can retain control even if they hold less than 50 percent of the shares. Retention of voting control can be accomplished by having a new class of common stock with limited voting rights. However, such stock may have limited appeal to investors and may therefore sell for less than ordinary common stock.

- **Sharing Your Success.** By contributing their capital, investors share the risk of your business—and they also will share your success. But is their share of your success disproportionate? If you realistically anticipate unusually high earnings in the next two or three years, and you can obtain bank or other financing, you may wish temporarily to defer a public offering. Then, when you do go public, your shares will command a higher price.

- **Loss of Privacy.** Of all the changes that result when a company goes public, perhaps none is more troublesome than its loss of privacy. When a company becomes publicly held, it is required by the Securities and Exchange Commission (SEC) to disclose much information about your company—its sales, profit margins, and competitive position. It also will reveal highly sensitive information, such as compensation paid to key executives and directors, special incentives for management, and many of the plans and strategies that underlie the company's operations. While these disclosures need not include every detail of the company's operations, information that could significantly affect investors' decisions must be disclosed. These disclosures rarely harm your business. For the most part, employee compensation and the prices you pay for materials and receive for your products are governed by market forces—not by your disclosed financial results.

  Such information is required at the time of the initial public offering, and it normally will have to be updated on a continuing and timely basis thereafter.

  As a result of this loss of privacy, some companies feel that special arrangements with key personnel or other related parties that are normal for a private company but that might be misconstrued by outsiders should be discontinued.

- **Limiting Management's Freedom to Act.** By going public, management surrenders some degree of freedom. While the management of a privately held company generally is free to act by itself, the management of a public company must obtain the approval of the board of directors on certain major matters, and on special matters must even seek the consent of the shareholders. (Obtaining directors' approval or consent need not be a significant problem. The board of directors, if kept informed on a timely basis, can usually be counted on to understand management's needs, offer support, and grant much of the desired flexibility.)

- **Periodic Reporting.** As a public company, you will be subject to the periodic reporting requirements of the SEC.

These requirements include quarterly financial reporting (Form 10-Q), annual financial reporting (Form 10-K), prompt reporting of current material events (Form 8-K), and various other reporting requirements, such as those for sales of control shares (shares held by controlling shareholders) and tender offers. The various reporting requirements, which include audited financial statements, usually result in the need for more extensive and more timely financial and other information. This may require improved accounting systems, more accounting staff, and increased use of lawyers, auditors, and other outside advisors. Securities analysts and the financial press also will make demands on your time and that of your executives. In short, some costs of doing business will increase. As more fully explained in Chapter 8, the SEC provides some relief to small business issuers by providing more simplified quarterly and annual reporting requirements.

- **Initial and Ongoing Expenses.** Going public can be costly and will result in a tremendous commitment of management's time and energy. The largest single cost in an initial public offering is the underwriter's discount or commission, which generally ranges from 6 percent to 10 percent of the offering price. In addition, legal and accounting fees, printing costs, the underwriter's out-of-pocket expenses (generally not included in the commission), filing fees, and registrar and transfer agent fees can typically add another $300,000 to $500,000 to the cost of an offering of $5 million to $10 million. Costs depend upon factors such as the complexity of the registration statement, the extent to which legal counsel must be involved, the familiarity of management with the reporting necessary of a public company, and the availability of audited financial statements for recent years. These expenses generally are not deductible for income tax purposes. On the other hand, they also do not affect your reported net income, because they are considered by Generally Accepted Accounting Principles (GAAP) to be part of a capital transaction and are therefore deducted from the proceeds of the offering.

Beyond the initial offering, there are the continuing costs of the periodic reports and proxy statements filed with regulatory agencies and distributed to shareholders, and the increased professional fees paid to attorneys, accountants, registrars, and transfer agents for additional services. The time management will spend preparing the ongoing reports and statements also must be considered, because this responsibility will divert its attention from managing operations.

The company also may need to upgrade its management and accounting information systems to enable it to maintain adequate financial records and systems of internal accounting controls to meet the accounting provisions of the Foreign Corrupt Practices Act, which are included in the Securities Exchange Act of 1934. Upgraded systems also may be necessary to report timely financial information.

- **Shareholders' Expectations.** Investors generally will expect you to maintain and continually improve your company's performance with respect to measures such as revenue, earnings, growth, and market share. Should the investors become disillusioned with your performance, your share price will suffer. Thus, you may be tempted to try to compromise long-term profitability in the interest of maintaining annual and quarterly reported results. Some shareholders will expect dividends when you may believe the company would be best served by reinvesting earnings. These shareholder pressures are real and must be weighed carefully. But a sound business strategy, adequately disclosed and explained to shareholders, may mitigate any adverse market reaction.

- **Restrictions on Selling Existing Shareholders' Shares.** Controlling or major shareholders of a public company are not free to sell their shares at will. The SEC has restrictions on when and how many shares insiders may sell. You must be aware of these restrictions when you plan an initial public offering and the number of existing shareholders' shares (secondary offering) to be sold at that time. Additionally, under penalty of civil and criminal law, no one with inside information about your company may trade in its stock before that information becomes public. Other restrictions include the short-swing profit provisions, which require that certain insiders who realize a gain on your stock within six months of its purchase return that gain to the company, whether or not the trading was based on inside information.

- **Fiduciary Responsibilities.** As the owner of a private business, the money you invested and risked was your own. As the manager of a public company, the money you invest and risk is that of the shareholders. You are accountable to them, so you must approach potential conflicts of interest with the utmost caution. It also will be necessary to work with your board of directors to help them discharge their fiduciary responsibilities when acting on corporate matters.

2

THE DECISION
TO GO PUBLIC

You have objectively weighed the benefits and drawbacks of going public, both for your company and its major shareholders. And you believe, perhaps still tentatively, that the interests of your company and shareholders would best be served by a public offering. But is the timing right for you to go public? Is your company ready and will it generate sufficient interest? Are initial public offerings in general, and in your industry in particular, performing well in the marketplace? You may wonder whether you should investigate alternative sources of financing and defer a public offering to a more opportune time. If so, you still need to know what preparations should be undertaken now in anticipation of an initial public offering in the future.

Your response to these questions can be key to both the success of an initial public offering and the ongoing performance of your shares in the after market.

IS THIS THE TIME?

Suppose you have weighed all the pros and cons, and have decided that the best thing for the company is to go public. But when? Timing is crucial and raises several questions.

11

Is now the best time to go public? If needed capital is available from nonpublic sources at reasonable cost, you may want to delay going public. If funds raised from other sources can be used to increase the company's growth potential, the value of the company's stock may increase. At a later date, the increased stock value may result in raising more capital or selling fewer shares.

Are your plans in order? After the offering, the stock's price may decline unless the company continues to show good progress and profits. A well-developed strategic business plan (including a multiyear financial plan) can help minimize adverse surprises by identifying the critical elements for continued success and providing benchmarks against which to monitor the company's progress.

The most obvious risk is that the offering will not be completed and the costs that have been incurred will have gone for nothing. This may occur because changes in the market or disappointing financial results cause the underwriter to back out. Another risk is that the stock may have to be offered at a lower price per share to attract investors. This will either result in lower proceeds from the offering or greater dilution to current shareholders.

What Are the Risks of Going Public at the Wrong Time?

Timing can be everything. Offerings that would not have been underwritten one year have taken the market by storm the following year. Determining the optimal time for your company to go public depends on many factors: the urgency of your financial need, the availability of alternative financing sources, capital market conditions for your industry, and the market's predisposition toward new issues in general.

Even offerings that sell enthusiastically can fail in the aftermarket, particularly if subsequent operating results are less than anticipated. A company that loses credibility in the financial community faces a long, difficult process in regaining investors' confidence, and a stock that loses value also can be vulnerable to shareholders' lawsuits.

IS YOUR COMPANY READY?

This may be one of the most difficult questions to answer. There is no formula or universal rule to determine whether a company is sufficiently large, mature, or profitable to go public. A review of recent successful offerings, however, can provide some useful generalizations about what investors look for in a newly public company.

Size

Various underwriters have their own rules of thumb for what constitutes an adequate size to support a public offering. These are based primarily on revenue and net earnings. Generally, investors most readily accept companies that are growing and have revenue of at least $20 million or more and net earnings of at least $1 million. But the exceptions are almost as commonplace as the rule. In recent years, a sizable number of initial public offerings have come from start-up companies with minimal revenue, many of which have never shown a profit. But these start-up companies normally have other appeals—such as an innovative new product with a potentially significant market and a proven management team—to compensate for the lack of a financial track record.

Management

Now is the time, before the decision is irreversible, for management to analyze itself. Can it comfortably adjust to the loss of the relative freedom to act as it sees fit and to the loss of privacy? Are senior executives ready to cope with the public's scrutiny of the company's actions? Are they ready to admit outsiders to the decision-making process? Do they have the leadership capability to grow as the company grows? Does management command credibility in the financial community?

A strong, capable management team is one of the key ingredients underwriters and investors look for in a prospective public company. The management team of a public company will have significant new responsibilities. In addition to managing the business aspects of a growing company, the management team must deal effectively with outside financial and credit analysts, the financial press, and public shareholders. Investors may be wary of the team's ability to deal with these new complexities. In such cases, it is not unusual for a company to hire a key financial executive with a proven track record in taking a company public. The offer of shares or stock options in a prospective public company often helps attract a top executive who is known to the financial community and can thus boost management credibility.

Growth

Investors look for both a record of consistently high growth and a demonstrated potential for continuing that growth in the future. If the momentum is not there when the company goes public, investors will turn to more promising opportunities, and the offering may fizzle. Having a new or innovative product, a significant market share or proven potential in a new market, and being part of an emerging industry all contribute to your prospects, real and perceived, for growth. Again, there are exceptions to the general rule.

Many companies with a good track record of stable revenue and earnings have made successful public offerings. In these cases, investors may trade off prospects for exceptional growth and price appreciation for lower risk and a reliable dividend stream.

There are no hard-and-fast rules, but some underwriters will not consider taking a company public unless it can point to revenue of at least $20 million and annual net income of $1 million, with anticipated growth of 15 percent to 25 percent a year for the next few years. There are exceptions, such as new companies in the glamour industries. Each company must consider its own circumstances, bearing in mind that few elements in the overall picture will impress the investor as much as momentum.

Information Systems

A public company is required to provide timely and reliable financial information to investors. If the company's management and accounting information systems are inadequate, now is the time to get them in first-class working order. There are legal liabilities for reporting false or misleading information, not to mention the loss of investors' confidence if information is not timely and accurate.

Use of Proceeds

The amount of the offering and the use to which the proceeds will be applied also are evaluated by both underwriters and investors. The amount of the offering must be predicated not only on "what you can get," but on your specific financing needs. Cash flow forecasts and capital expenditure projections are useful tools to help you determine your financing needs, and your independent auditors can assist you in their preparation.

Underwriters and investors consider all of the above factors in evaluating your company, but weaknesses in any of these areas need not preclude a public offering. Investors often will accept trade-offs in size, track record, and growth prospects. The single issue on which they rarely will compromise is management strength.

If you still think your company lacks the size or earnings to support a successful public offering, there are other avenues to explore. You might consider merging with another company in your industry that also is too small for an initial public offering. Such a merger could result in an amalgamated company whose combined assets, earnings, and management will make a public offering feasible.

The considerations must be weighed carefully—a premature public offering may have serious long-term consequences. If your company falters shortly after going public—whether because of unstable management, technological difficulties, or market forces—its credibility will be undermined. You may even find your company and its executives subject to litigation by disgruntled shareholders. Regaining investor confidence will be difficult.

IS THE MARKET READY?

The market for initial offerings has varied dramatically from the depressed levels of the mid-1970s, when fewer than 50 companies a year went public, to record highs of over 500 companies in the early 1990s. In deciding whether this is the right time to go public, one of the critical questions is whether the mood of the market is right. Is the market strong or slumping? Are prices rising or falling? Is trading volume up or down?

Market conditions can change rapidly. Many factors influence the market—political developments, interest rates, inflation, economic forecasts, and sundry matters that seem unrelated to the quality of your stock. The market is admittedly emotional, and investors' moods change from bullish to bearish and back again to the consternation of everyone, even the experts. Investor acceptance of new issues is cyclical, but often not predictable. Investor infatuation with a certain industry can significantly increase the share price that can be obtained. But the "window" for new issues, and for your industry in particular, can unexpectedly close just as quickly as it opened. A complex, ever-changing capital market virtually necessitates the advice of an underwriter or investment banker in determining the optimal time to go public. When the market is favorable, many companies go to the market to obtain funds that they will not need until some time in the future, thereby eliminating the need to speculate on future market conditions.

ADVANCE PLANNING

Planning for a public offering of securities should start now. Whether you are considering going public within the next six months or in three years, you will have to consider a variety of factors. Early attention to these planning considerations can help reduce many of the costs and burdens of an initial public offering. Starting now to lay the groundwork for a strong corporate image and long-term investor interest will pay future dividends in the form of a stronger and more stable aftermarket for your shares.

Corporate Housekeeping—Questions to Be Considered

After you have decided to take your company public, consider the steps needed to ensure a smooth transition from private to public company. You may need to do some corporate housekeeping. You will have to determine whether the necessary information for the registration statement is available and, if not, make plans to assemble it.

Corporate housekeeping generally begins during the planning stage and may not be completed until the registration statement is filed with the SEC. You should consider whether the existing corporate, capital, and management structures are appropriate for a public company and whether transactions with owners and management have been properly documented and recorded. The following are typical questions to be considered during this phase:

- Should the company's capital structure be changed? Restructuring may have tax implications, but you can mitigate any tax disadvantages with appropriate planning. You may want to simplify it by issuing common shares in exchange for preferred stock or special classes of common stock.
- Should additional shares of stock be authorized? Additional shares might be needed for the public offering or for future acquisitions or sales.
- Should the stock be split before you go public? To improve the common stock's marketability, after consultation with underwriters, companies frequently split their stock so that

the offering price of the stock will be between $10 to $20 per share.

- Should affiliated companies be combined? A public company generally is organized as a single corporation, perhaps with subsidiaries. Affiliated companies might provide services to each other, compete with each other, or sell related products and services. The combined entity may well be more attractive to investors and thus command a higher price in the market.

- Should the company's articles of incorporation or bylaws be amended? A private company may have special voting provisions that are inappropriate for a public company, or it might be desirable to establish certain committees of the board of directors, such as audit and compensation committees.

- Are the company's stock records accurate and current? Accurate shareholder information is a must for a public company. (While reviewing the stock records, be alert for problems with previous issuances of unregistered securities.)

- Are the company's transactions or arrangements with the owners and members of management appropriate for a public company, and are they adequately documented? The SEC requires public companies to fully disclose all significant related-party transactions. In this regard, they should be identified and discussed with the company's legal counsel early in the process. For example, certain arrangements with shareholders and officers may serve a private company well, but could be considered inappropriate for a public company. Your legal counsel can assist you in challenging the appropriateness of your contractual obligations by performing a "legal audit" of significant contracts, including:

  Employment Contracts
  Stock Option or Purchase Plans
  Debt and Lease Agreements
  Shareholder or Management Loans

    Rights of First Refusal

    Corporate Charter and Bylaws

    Major Supply Contracts

- Have important contracts and employment agreements been put in writing? Do they need to be amended? Should a stock-option plan be implemented? Should additional options be granted under existing plans?

- Does management possess sufficient depth and experience for a public company? The company may need to supplement or upgrade its financial and/or operating management before it goes public. Changes in the board of directors are often appropriate, for example, adding outside directors.

Never Too Soon

Strong relationships with professional advisors can be a significant asset for a private company. For a public company, they are crucial. It is never too soon to start developing those relationships.

You already may have an investment banker. If not, now is the time to develop such a relationship. They range from large, full-service investment banking firms to individuals specializing in specific industries. Investment bankers can advise you on available sources of capital and on the desirability of offering securities at a given time, both with respect to initial offerings in general and in your industry in particular. Through them you can keep your finger on the pulse of the capital markets. Often the same firm that serves as your investment banker can also act as your underwriter when you decide to go public. Therefore, in selecting an investment banker, you also should consider the factors relevant to the selection of underwriters, which is more fully discussed in Chapter 4.

Preparing to be a public company also may necessitate some changes in your internal reporting and in the way your company is managed. In many private companies, the officers report informally to the president, who makes the final decisions on significant matters. A public company requires more formalized management. The ultimate transition will be more orderly if you start now to manage your company in the style of a public company.

Selecting the best people to serve on the board of directors can be one of the most important tasks of a company that has decided to go public. This decision can affect the short- and long-term direction of the company, as well as the success of the initial public offering.

Board members will play a key role in assuring the development of a strategic plan, bringing their experience and new ideas into the company, monitoring the chief executive officer's performance, assuring the integrity of company operations, and counseling top management. In addition, they will directly impact future mergers and acquisitions, tender offers, compensation of top management, selection of senior executives, and many of the company's capital expenditures.

Ideally, the board of directors should begin to play a larger role in policy decisions for a period of two to three years in advance of going public. This often represents a major change for an emerging company that traditionally has been run by one or a small group of entrepreneurs. However, this change should be made, as it provides evidence to underwriters and investors of stability and maturity, and is one indication that your company is less likely to struggle in the new public environment.

The board of directors should be structured in a way that promotes the board's role as an independent and knowledgeable overseer of the company's affairs and performance. There is no single board structure that can be prescribed for all companies that have decided to go public. Nonetheless, there are many factors that should be considered when assembling a board for a company that is contemplating going public.

Participation as a board member can be a significant time and legal commitment to the company and its shareholders. Accordingly, an individual lends his or her name and reputation to the integrity of the company when agreeing to become a board member.

Companies going public often try to identify individuals with strong credentials in their industry, other areas of the business community, or public service as candidates for directors, because the reputation of board members will be carefully evaluated by underwriters and some investors; however, companies considering such individuals sometimes find them reluctant to assume such a role due to the liability they must assume under the 1933 Act when they only have limited familiarity with the company. Under the Securities Act of 1933 (1933 Act), a director can be held liable if the registration statement contains any untrue statement of a material fact or fails to state a material fact that was required. As today's boards face the growing risk of litigation, companies are finding new ways to legally protect their directors. In addition to paying increasing premiums for Directors and Officers (D&O) liability insurance coverage, many companies are changing their corporate charters to permit indemnification of directors. While the SEC historically has not favored indemnification for securities law violations, the majority of public companies obtain D&O insurance for directors and have amended their corporate charters to permit indemnification of directors.

Appendix B includes a discussion of the typical organization of the board of directors including types of committees and board member compensation.

The prospectus* for your initial public offering generally must include audited financial statements for the past three years, although that requirement is reduced in certain circumstances, such as for small business issuers under Regulation S-B. It also may require selected financial information for the last five years. These disclosure requirements apply only for the years your company has been in existence. A company usually will not be allowed to go public if its financial statements have not been audited. In some cases, a two- or three-year audit can be performed in anticipation of a public offering, but even then it may cause unforeseen delays and turn up unexpected adjustments to earnings.

---

*The prospectus discloses information about the company and the offering and is distributed as a separate document or booklet to prospective investors.

As a public company, you will be subject to certain SEC disclosure requirements, such as specified data by industry segment. To prepare for this, you should make sure your financial reporting system can provide the necessary data. Have your auditors review this data. Many companies' internal reporting systems already provide industry segment data in some form, but the method they use probably does not correspond to that prescribed by the SEC or Financial Accounting Standards Board (FASB) Statement No. 14, "Segment Reporting." You should consider these various requirements early, with the assistance of your independent auditors. By making the necessary changes in accounting practices now, you can avoid the inconvenience of having to implement them as you go public, or having to delay your offering.

A company also can run into problems if, in the two or three years preceding a public offering, it acquires a significant business not previously audited. Because these unaudited subsidiary statements can affect the consolidated financial statements, and also because of the SEC requirement to provide separate audited financial statements for significant acquired companies, a company that makes such an acquisition can be precluded from going public until such information is available. Therefore, if you are considering a public offering of securities in the next two or three years, you will want to keep audit requirements in mind when you plan any acquisitions.

Many private companies have annual audits performed even if not otherwise required and are therefore in a position to go public on short notice. An audit also improves the credibility and reliability of your financial statements and will help you deal with external lenders and suppliers and improve internal management information. Another benefit of an audit is that your independent auditors gain knowledge of your business that helps them come up with creative solutions to your business needs. These ideas, communicated both in personal meetings and in management letters, recommend ways to improve your operations, including cost-effective ways to improve internal controls. Effective and timely internal financial reporting and a good system of internal controls are important for public companies, just as they are for a private company.

In addition to providing audit and other advisory services, your auditors will help determine whether your accounting practices are appropriate for a public company. Sometimes, SEC interpretations of generally accepted accounting principles (GAAP) may necessitate a change in accounting practices and disclosures by a company about to go public. Alternatively, companies may desire to change their accounting policies to conform their accounting policies to those more commonly used by other public companies in their industry and thereby enhance the value of the offering. By making the necessary changes now, you can avoid the distractions of having to do so as you go public. Such changes also might have tax implications, so you will want to address tax planning considerations early.

Once your company is publicly held, the SEC sets limits on the sale of "restricted" stock (generally shares issued in private placements) and any shares held by controlling shareholders. Existing shareholders may sell any portion of their holdings without technical restriction as part of the initial public offering. The only restriction then is a practical concern that the offering not be perceived as a bailout of existing shareholders. However, if one of the goals of the public offering is to make existing shareholders' shares salable in the aftermarket, advance planning can reduce the impact of these SEC restrictions. The specifics of these SEC rules are summarized in Chapter 6. Consult your attorneys for guidance on structuring these plans to conform with the SEC's rules and interpretations. Note, however, that restricted shares may always be sold through another public offering.

A Year before the Offering

Selling your shares and maintaining investor interest in the aftermarket is not dissimilar from selling your products or services to customers. Both are aided by name recognition, advertising and publicity, a product support system, and good distribution channels. Your underwriter and the underwriting syndicate will provide the distribution channels. However, you need to create your corporate image and build the foundation for a strong investor relations program.

Creating your corporate image takes time, so you should start well in advance of the public offering. Bear in mind, too, that the SEC imposes restrictions on new forms of advertising or publicity you may engage in once you have started the registration process by retaining an underwriter.

The first step in creating a public image is to perform a thorough self-evaluation of your company and its future. Consider your potential geographic appeal. Depending on the nature of your product and your geographic product market area, your shares may be limited to a regional market, or they might attract national or even international interest.

In what industry will your company be categorized? That could bear on your company's appeal to investors. Certain industries are more attractive to investors than others, and thus command a higher price-earnings ratio. If your business could be classified in more than one way, aim for the industry classification that would result in the highest price-earnings ratio. Some companies with diverse product lines may be identified only with one of their better-known products. A good publicity campaign can create a broader based image for your company.

Also consider what types of investors you can or wish to attract. There are obvious advantages to luring institutional investors—they control a hefty portion of America's investment capital. But they also often have various technical investment restrictions relating to, for example, the number and price of your shares on the market, earnings history, dividend policy, and stock exchange listing. These restrictions initially may limit your company's institutional appeal, or they may spur you to take steps to improve it.

Once you have determined your target market of investors and the corporate image you wish to project, you must find ways to reach that market. You may wish to hire a financial public relations firm and prepare a corporate brochure describing your company, its products, markets, and operations. If you already engage in product advertising, your advertising campaigns might include a corporate focus to help build investor interest in your company.

Try to identify the securities analysts and members of the business media who follow your industry and make a special effort to reach them, either through a personal meeting or by including them on your mailing list. Building a good relationship with the press, both trade publications and the national or local business and financial press, will help keep publicity flowing during and after your public offering.

Compensation Strategies

As you prepare your company to go public, you will need to take certain steps with respect to compensation. Even if your company has an effective compensation program already in place, you should reexamine it as you prepare for your initial public offering (IPO). Although you can—and in many cases should—preserve elements from your existing compensation plans, you will need to adapt them to suit your new status as a public company.

As a public company, you have a powerful new element for your company's compensation plans: publicly traded equity—both in the form of outright stock grants and in the form of stock options. On the other hand, you will be making compensation decisions in a more public arena. In this new environment, you will need to communicate your pay policies not only to employees, but to regulators, stock exchange officials, investors, and the public at large. Therefore, in establishing your compensation strategies, you should consider the factors which are more fully discussed in Appendix G.

Evaluate Your System of Internal Control

Many companies have long recognized the importance of strong internal controls. An effective internal control structure can help companies achieve established financial goals, prevent loss of resources, and prepare reliable financial statements.

Companies considering an IPO and the requirements that result need to take a close look at their systems of internal control and evaluate their effectiveness.

The importance of internal controls became clear with the enactment of the Foreign Corrupt Practices Act of 1977 (FCPA). The FCPA was a direct result of investigation and a public scandal that revealed that over 400 U.S. companies had secretly made kickbacks, bribes, or other questionable payments to foreign officials to obtain or maintain business connections.

There are two major provisions to the FCPA, the first of which affects all U.S. companies. Under the FCPA, it is illegal for any U.S. business to pay or authorize payment of anything of value to foreign officials to obtain or maintain business relationships. As a result of the provisions of this part of the FCPA, many companies have established written codes of conduct to address these issues.

The other major provision of the FCPA, which relates to accounting issues, applies only to companies that file reports with the SEC under the Securities Exchange Act of 1934 (1934 Act). Two major requirements are mandated by the accounting provisions of the FCPA. One is that registrants establish and maintain books, records, and accounts that accurately reflect the transactions of the registrant. Second, registrants are required to establish a system of internal controls adequate to meet the following four requirements:

- Transactions are executed in accordance with management's general or specific authorization.

- Transactions are recorded as necessary (1) to permit preparation of financial statements in conformity with GAAP or any other criteria applicable to such statements, and (2) to maintain accountability for assets.

- Access to assets is permitted only in accordance with management's authorization.

- The recorded accountability for assets is compared with the existing assets at reasonable intervals and appropriate action is taken with respect to any differences.

The accounting provisions of the FCPA, which are the responsibility of management, amend the 1934 Act and are subject to SEC enforcement.

PREPARING YOUR BUSINESS PLAN

Whether you decide to go public or pursue alternative financing, you cannot succeed without a sound business plan. A business plan is a valuable management tool that can be utilized in a wide variety of situations. In most companies, business plans are used at a minimum to:

- Set the goals and objectives for the company's performance.
- Provide a basis for evaluating and controlling the company's performance.
- Communicate a company's message to middle managers, outside directors, suppliers, lenders, and potential investors.

When utilized most efficiently, the same business plan, with slight modification, can be used for all three purposes.

Setting Goals and Objectives

The business plan for an early-stage company is, in many ways, a first attempt at strategic planning. An entrepreneur should use a business plan as a tool for setting the direction of a company over the next several years, and a plan should set the action steps and processes to guide the company through this period. Many entrepreneurs say that the pressures of the day-to-day management of a company leave them little time for planning, and this is unfortunate since, without it, an owner runs the risk of proceeding blindly through the rapidly changing business environment. Writing a business plan does not guarantee a particular business environment, nor is it a guarantee that problems will not arise. But, with a thoroughly thought-out plan, a business owner can better anticipate a crisis situation and deal with it up front. Further, a well-constructed plan may help avoid certain problems altogether. All in all, business planning is probably more important to the survival of a small and growing company than a larger, more mature one.

Performance Benchmarks

A business plan can also be used to develop and document milestones along your business's path to success. In the heat of daily operations, you may find that taking an objective look at the performance of your business is difficult. Often, the trees encountered daily obscure your view of the forest in which your company operates. A business plan can provide you and your management team with an objective basis for determining if the business is on track to meet the goals and objectives you have set.

Internal and External Communications

Your company's story must be told and retold many times to prospective investors, potential and new employees, outside advisors, and potential customers. The most important part of the story is the part about the future, the part featured in a business plan.

Your business plan should show how all of the pieces of your company fit together to create a vibrant organization capable of meeting its goals and objectives. It must be able to communicate your company's distinctive competence to anyone who might have an interest.

The steps you should follow in preparing your business plan whether you are writing it for the first time or rewriting it for the twentieth follow.

1. **Identify Your Objectives.** Before you can write a successful business plan, you must determine who will read the plan, what they already know about your company, what they want to know about your company, how they intend to use the information they will find in the plan. The needs of your target audience must be combined with your communication objectives—what you want the reader to know. Once you have identified and resolved any conflicts between what your target audience wants to know and what you want them to know, you are ready to begin preparing a useful business plan.

2. **Outline Your Business Plan.** Once you have identified the objectives for your business plan, and you know the areas that you want to emphasize, you prepare an outline based on these special requirements. The outline can be as general or detailed as you wish, but typically a detailed outline will be more useful to you while you are writing your plan.

3. **Review Your Outline.** Review your outline to identify the areas that, based on your readers and objectives, should be presented in detail or summary form in your business plan. Keep in mind that your business plan should describe your company at a fairly high level and that extremely detailed descriptions are to be avoided in most cases. However, you must be prepared to provide detailed support for your statements and assumptions apart from your business plan if necessary.

4. **Write Your Plan.** The order in which the specific elements of the plan are developed will vary depending on the age of your company and your experience in preparing business plans.

   You will probably find it necessary to research many areas before you have enough information to write about them. Most people begin by collecting historical financial information about their company and/or industry and completing their market research before beginning to write any part of their plan. Even though you may do extensive research before you begin to develop your plan, you may find that additional research is required before you complete it. You should take the time to complete the required research because many of the assumptions and strategies described in the plan will be based on your findings and analysis.

Initial drafts of prospective financial statements are often prepared next, after the basic financial and market research and analysis are completed. By preparing these statements at this time, you will have a good idea which strategies will work from a financial perspective before investing many hours in writing a detailed description of them. As you develop your prospective statements, be certain you keep detailed notes on the assumptions you make to facilitate preparation of the footnotes that must accompany the statements, as well as the composition of other business plan elements.

The last element of a business plan to be prepared is the Executive Summary. Since it is a summary of the plan, its contents are contingent on the rest of the document, and it cannot be written properly until the other components of the plan are essentially complete.

While preparing each element of your plan, refer to the outline in Appendix F to be certain that you have covered each area thoroughly.

5. **Have Your Plan Reviewed.** Once you have completed and reviewed a draft of your plan, have someone familiar with business management and the planning process review it for completeness (by referring to the outline in this publication), objectivity, logic, presentation, and effectiveness as a communications tool. Then, modify your plan based on your reviewer's comments.

6. **Update Your Plan.** Business plans are "living" documents and must be periodically updated or they become useless. As your environment and objectives—and those of your

readers—change, update your plan to reflect these changes. Refer to this booklet each time your plan is updated to be certain that all areas are properly covered.

See Appendix F for an outline of suggested items to include in a business plan.

Financial Information

Financial statements and projections for the next three to five years generally are included here. Financial modeling often is used to present alternative "what-if" scenarios.

This is the point of the business plan—how much money you need, how it will be used, when you need it, whether you might need more, and when and how you can repay the money.

Some parts of the plan are reasonably easy to prepare, while others require more time and effort, and often some research. You will want to retain the advice and assistance of your auditors and attorneys, either in preparing or reviewing the document.

ALTERNATIVES TO GOING PUBLIC

As part of the process of deciding whether and when to go public, you will want to consider not only the costs and consequences of a public offering, but also the relative merits of alternative sources of financing. The selection of alternative sources of capital will depend on the urgency of your financial need, corporate and shareholder objectives, the amount of capital needed, the use to which the proceeds will be applied, and the relative size and maturity of your company. The following alternatives are discussed in greater detail in Chapter 7.

Private Placements and Limited Offerings

The SEC has established exemptions from federal registration for sales of securities meeting various conditions. These conditions relate to the amount of capital raised (up to $1 million, up to $5 million, and unlimited amounts) and the number and financial sophistication of investors who purchase the securities (from an unlimited number to only 35 "nonaccredited" investors plus unlimited "accredited" investors). Various other conditions relate to prohibitions on advertising, disclosure requirements, and resale restrictions.

Intrastate Offerings

To promote local financing of local business, the SEC exempts from registration offerings made only to the residents of the state in which the issuer resides and carries on its business. This exemption is not restricted with respect to amount or purchasers, but a number of other conditions are imposed. The company must be incorporated in the state and must carry out a significant portion of its business there. In addition, the purchasers must be residents of the state. Out-of-state resale of the shares is restricted. Although the SEC's registration requirement would not apply to an intrastate offering, the requirements of the state in which the company is domiciled must be adhered to.

Commercial Lenders and Lessors

Loans from banks, insurance companies and other financial institutions, or lease financing are the most common ways to raise capital. The relative ease of obtaining a bank loan or lease financing makes these sources well suited to short-term working capital needs and equipment financing. Semipermanent capital to purchase real property or to make acquisitions also may be available from banks and insurance companies. However, the availability of financing from commercial lenders and lessors may require collateral or personal guarantees. You also may have to maintain certain financial measures while the debt or lease is outstanding. Debt financing also commits your company to cash outflows that may be hard to meet if interest rates climb or if your business declines.

Strategic Partnerships

You can obtain the resources to meet your economic and strategic goals by forming an alliance with a larger, financially stronger company. A strategic partnership can contribute more than money to your company's success. For example, your partner might provide manufacturing or technological capabilities, or give your company access to new or expanded distribution channels.

Employee Stock Ownership Plans

Consider an employee stock ownership plan (ESOP) if, in addition to raising capital, your goals include increased liquidity, estate planning, and employee motivation. An ESOP is a tax-favored type of employee benefit plan that provides a vehicle for employee ownership of a company by allowing the ESOP to borrow money to purchase your stock and maintain it for your employees' retirement.

Government Loans and Guarantees

Although subject to a variety of qualifications, restrictions, and delays, government loans and guarantees are often a very attractive source of financing. Some very reasonable rates and repayment schedules can be obtained. These programs sometimes represent the only available source of financing for both start-up small businesses and larger businesses falling on hard times. A variety of programs are available at the federal, state, and local levels.

Venture Capitalists

Raising capital through venture capitalists or other institutional equity investors can be either the first step in going public or an alternative to going public. Venture capitalists typically will agree to provide a significant portion of your capital needs, but in return they require a significant and, frequently, controlling equity interest in your business and direct representation on your board of directors. They typically invest in businesses with relatively high risk in the hope of high returns. Their involvement in the management of your company can range from passive monitoring of results to hands-on involvement in day-to-day operations. Financing with a venture capitalist almost invariably results in ownership dilution, and often in immediate or eventual loss of control.

Sale or Merger

If your motivation for considering a public offering is to liquidate your investment, selling or merging your company may be an attractive alternative. Other corporations or your company's existing management team may be attracted to the opportunities of your company. Your decision to sell depends on your personal goals, but to maximize your own returns, you should consider this alternative.

3

WHO GETS INVOLVED

While the ultimate responsibility for going public falls on your company, the success of an initial public offering depends on a coordinated team effort involving your company's executives, auditors, attorneys, underwriters, and even your financial printer. Your professional advisors play a big part in helping you evaluate your options and plan for a public offering. Their job becomes even more important as you begin the actual registration process. Finally, the role of the SEC cannot be overlooked.

YOUR COMPANY'S EXECUTIVES

Starting with that first pivotal decision—whether to go public—your company's executives play a central role in the planning, execution, and continuing success of a public offering. They have the primary responsibility, perhaps with assistance from a financial public relations firm, for creating your company's public image. As a result, they may have to spend a great deal of time meeting trade analysts, members of the financial press, and other targeted individuals considered influential in creating your public image.

Your company's executives must select the professional advisors best qualified to assist the company as it goes public. They must initiate all of the necessary advance preparations and work with your advisors in carrying out those preparations. Although aided by professional advice and assistance, they are the ones who make the many important decisions and carry out the variety of tasks that precede the offering.

Your executives will meet with the auditors, attorneys, and underwriters to plan the timetable for the registration process and allocate the responsibilities. After that, they will meet frequently with some or all of these advisors at critical junctures in the process. Your executives will have to accumulate much of the detailed information required in the registration statement. They also will have to review the schedules and other information prepared by the auditors and attorneys.

Once the registration statement is filed with the SEC and you wait for the registration statement to "go effective," your executives most likely will be taken on a "road show" by your managing underwriters. This tour, discussed in more detail in Chapter 5, gives the underwriting syndicate, potential investors, and securities analysts an opportunity to meet your company's management, hear their presentations, and ask questions about the company and the information in the prospectus.

In short, big demands will be made on management's time before, during, and after the public offering. Management must be prepared for these responsibilities and be capable of assuming them. The strength of your management team will be scrutinized closely by underwriters and investors alike. Management represents your company to the financial community.

YOUR AUDITORS

Your independent auditors play a significant and varied role in the complex process of going public, so you will want to select an experienced professional services firm that can offer the specialized services required by a company embarking on its initial public offering. Most companies choose a firm with a strong national reputation as well as experience in securities offerings and in dealing with the SEC. Having highly capable auditors on your team of professional advisors not only will help you avoid costly delays and errors in the registration process, but will provide you with continuing counsel and assistance in dealing with the many SEC reporting and other obligations of a public company.

Your auditors should become involved in the early stages of a public offering. They will help you assess the relative advantages and disadvantages of going public, advise you on alternative sources of financing, and help you investigate those alternatives. They also will advise you on both corporate and personal tax implications and estate planning considerations. They can help you assess and approach underwriters and advise you on negotiating with them.

Your auditors also will help you prepare one of the most important aspects of the prospectus—the financial disclosure package. For an established private company, the historical audited financial statements and financial highlights are the evidence of your size and earnings record. Depending on the nature of your offering, you may also prepare cash flow analyses, sensitivity studies, industry and competition studies, and marketing analyses. Your auditors can help you prepare and present that information clearly, concisely, and in accordance with SEC rules and regulations. They also will anticipate SEC concerns so that you can address these prior to the initial filing.

In addition to the SEC's financial statement requirements discussed previously, companies are required to present a summary of selected financial data for a period of five years (not required for small business issuers) and some underwriters prefer that all years listed be audited. In addition, many SEC disclosures and interpretations of GAAP may differ from those of private companies and therefore require careful consideration in preparing a public offering. These SEC interpretations can necessitate significant changes in the financial information you present. This underscores again the importance of establishing a relationship with a professional services firm well in advance of a public offering and of having annual audits performed.

Your auditors typically will provide "comfort letters" requested by your underwriters, which the underwriters will rely on as part of their "due diligence" (a concept discussed in

Chapter 5) with respect to certain financial information contained in the prospectus and registration statement.

Both before and after a public offering, a professional services firm offering a wide range of services can act as a key outside business advisor, monitoring almost any aspect of your business and suggesting alternatives for improving the efficiency, effectiveness, and profitability of your operations. A full-service firm has the resources to provide a full range of accounting, auditing, tax advisory, and management consulting services. For example, they can help you assess your information system needs, assist in selecting and implementing the system, and train your staff in its use.

As your business advisors, they can help you develop and implement appropriate budgeting and planning processes. They can assist you in developing a cash reporting system, including cash requirements forecasting, and can provide other cash management suggestions to help control your interest costs. Human resources specialists at the firm can help you determine the most effective organizational structure to anticipate the demands of being a public company. They can assist you in developing criteria and qualifications for new key executives, and advise you on competitive, tax-efficient compensation packages to attract and retain talented executives. And, on a personal level, experienced tax professionals in public accounting firms can help shareholders and management plan the most tax-effective way to meet their personal and family financial goals.

A good working relationship with your professional services firm, developed early, not only will facilitate the registration process but will prove valuable as you become a mature public company.

YOUR ATTORNEYS

Your attorneys will play an instrumental role in helping you prepare and execute your public offering. Their primary responsibility is to assist you in complying with all applicable federal and state securities laws and regulations and to advise you on the selection of any exemptions for which you may be eligible. Because of the highly complex nature of securities law, it is important to select a firm with broad experience in securities law and handling initial public offerings. If your general counsel does not have the necessary SEC expertise, they may be able to recommend a firm that does. Your auditors can also advise you on the selection of experienced SEC counsel.

Your attorneys will assist you in the pre-public planning stages. They will review your existing contractual obligations and suggest any necessary changes and revisions. Your attorneys will help you amend your articles of incorporation and by-laws as necessary. Your attorneys will recommend and help implement any changes to your capital structure that may be required to facilitate the public offering and to minimize the effect of SEC restrictions on the sale of these "restricted" shares after you go public.

Attorneys often assume a coordinating role in the preparation of your prospectus and registration statement, working closely with your management team and other professional advisors. Your attorneys will coordinate all correspondence with the SEC staff. They will review the entire prospectus and registration statement and advise you on the type of information that is legally relevant. For certain parts of that information, they will advise you on the form of presentation and the procedures necessary to verify its accuracy.

Certain exemptions from registration include requirements dealing with the level of investors' financial sophistication. Your attorneys will help you establish that the investors meet those qualifications. They will also advise you on the method and extent of disclosure to prospective investors when the exemption does not specify required disclosures.

Throughout the registration process, and particularly while preparing the registration statement, you will be working closely with and relying heavily on your attorneys. Careful selection of attorneys will enhance the smooth completion of your registration.

The attorneys you select to assist you in the registration statement process are not necessarily the same as the company uses
as its general counsel. In fact, many companies will retain attorneys specifically to meet the requirements of being a public
company, while at the same time retaining its general counsel to
handle the company's routine corporate matters.

YOUR UNDERWRITERS

Your underwriters play the central role in actually selling your
securities. Your direct contact is your lead or managing underwriter. The managing underwriter will have the primary responsibility for determining the initial price of the shares to be
sold. Your shares are distributed through an underwriting syndicate—assembled by your managing underwriters—consisting
of a number of other underwriters who also sell the shares to
individual and institutional investors.

Few companies attempt to sell their own shares through a
public offering without the help of underwriters—and with
good reason. The underwriting syndicate has the distribution
channels, contacts, and experience to reach a much broader
group of investors, lend more credibility to your offering, and
target specific investors for whom your shares are likely to hold
the most investment appeal. It also has the resources to invest in
this time-consuming effort, as well as the expertise to avoid the
potential liabilities and other consequences that can result from
an improperly handled selling effort.

In addition to their primary role in the initial sales effort, underwriters typically play a significant role in maintaining a
strong and stable aftermarket for your securities. They serve as
over-the-counter market-makers for your shares, buying and
selling shares on the interdealer market and generally helping
maintain interest in your shares among analysts and investors.
The selection of lead underwriters is discussed in detail in
Chapter 4.

YOUR FINANCIAL PRINTER

The selection of a financial printer for your prospectus and registration statement is a seemingly mundane issue. However, an experienced financial printer contributes to the timeliness and efficiency of the registration process. Significant time demands are placed on the printer in the final stages of the registration process. Revised drafts are often required on a "same-day" basis, and the final prospectus is often printed the night before the registration statement becomes effective.

Your financial printer should have an up-to-date knowledge of SEC rules and requirements with respect to paper size, format, size of type, and related technical matters, as well as the specialized facilities to deal with the accuracy, timing and security needs of a public offering.*

THE SEC

The final step in the registration process, before your securities are sold, is to obtain clearance from the SEC. The SEC is not responsible for evaluating or regulating the quality of securities offered to the public. Rather, it attempts to protect the public interest by ensuring that adequate information is provided to prospective and current investors to allow them to evaluate the quality of your securities.

The SEC was established by Congress in 1934 in response to the stock market crash of 1929. The SEC administers federal securities legislation, including the 1933 Act and the 1934 Act.

---

*Once the SEC's Electronic Data Gathering, Analysis and Retrieval System (EDGAR) is fully operational, the registration statement that will be filed with the SEC will be required to be filed electronically. Therefore, either your financial printer or a member of your organization must have a thorough understanding of EDGAR. Your auditors, attorneys, and underwriters can assist you in choosing a financial printer.

- The 1933 Act (also known as the "Truth in Securities" Act) has two primary requirements. First, it requires most companies to register public offerings of securities with the SEC before they are sold to the public, and second the securities must be registered by filing a registration statement, which encompasses the prospectus and includes specified business and financial information about the company and the securities offered. The 1933 Act, to fulfill its second requirement, contains provisions that impose civil and criminal liabilities on any company or person involved in preparing a registration statement that, when it becomes effective, contains a material misstatement or omission. The provisions apply not only to controlling shareholders, directors, underwriters, and those corporate officers and others who sign the registration statement, but also to the experts whose opinions are included in the registration statement.

- The 1934 Act has a twofold purpose: To prevent unfair practices in securities markets and to provide for periodic reporting. By authority of the 1934 Act, the SEC regulates stock exchanges, brokers, and company insiders. It also controls proxy solicitation, annual reports to shareholders, and tender offers. Required periodic reporting takes the form of the annual Form 10-K or 10-KSB, the quarterly Form 10-Q or 10-QSB, and Form 8-K for timely disclosure of specified material events or corporate changes deemed to be of importance to shareholders.

When your registration statement is filed with the SEC, the Division of Corporation Finance rigorously reviews it for adequacy of disclosure and compliance with relevant legislation and regulations. Comments from the SEC staff are reported to you or your legal counsel by means of a "comment letter," and those comments must then be resolved to the satisfaction of the SEC staff before your registration statement can become effective and the securities can be sold.

If the prospectus and registration statement are well-prepared and without controversial issues, SEC staff clearance can sometimes take as little as six or seven weeks. The period between initial filing and clearance by the SEC staff also depends to some extent on the number of registration statements and other filings the SEC staff has to review at that particular time. If significant deficiencies or controversial issues not previously reviewed with the SEC are found in the registration statement, delays can result. Additionally, greater than average complexity of the registrant's activities or the transaction being registered may require additional review time or result in a greater number of comments. A complex registration statement may result in a larger review/revision process despite a lack of contentious issues, simply because more disclosure generally gives the SEC staff more to review and comment on, or is more difficult to understand. In this regard, the typical registration statement filed in connection with an IPO will receive at least two and frequently three comment letters from the SEC that must be addressed before the registration statement is declared effective.

4

UNDERWRITING
YOUR OFFERING

Appropriate selection of managing underwriters is a key ingredient for a successful initial public offering. For some small companies, the reputation of the underwriters can be one of the more important factors investors consider in evaluating your offering. A variety of firms actively underwrite initial public offerings, from major national investment bankers to smaller regional brokerage firms with investment banking divisions. Many of the smaller firms specialize in specific industries.

SELECTING YOUR UNDERWRITERS

Selecting the managing underwriters best suited to your situation should begin with a self-evaluation of your company and its future plans. Consider the current and potential market for your product. If your geographic coverage is national or international, it may be best to retain a national firm to capitalize on and enhance your corporate image in the United States and in select areas abroad. If your sales market is regional, a regional firm may be able to serve you equally well.

If your industry is specialized, you may want to seek underwriters who specialize in your industry. If you plan to diversify, through acquisition or internally, consider using an investment banking firm that also has experience in that new industry. You can avoid having to repeat the selection process by choosing underwriters that can fill both your current and anticipated needs, in the hope of building a long-term professional relationship.

The selection process is two-way: Not all underwriters may be interested in your offering. Some do not handle initial public offerings or are interested in offerings only above certain minimum amounts. Others may decline on the basis of their assessment of your company's or industry's future prospects. The underwriters' reputation hangs largely on the success of the offerings they underwrite. Because underwriters are compensated only if the offering is completed (except for any expense a company may have agreed to reimburse), they will not want to commit time and resources unless they are reasonably confident that the offering will be completed.

Before approaching underwriters, you should develop a formal business plan that describes your company and its products, past performance, and future plans. Your business plan will serve both as a brief introduction to your company and as a sales tool when approaching the underwriter. The quality of your business plan will influence the underwriters' initial assessment of your company and its prospects, so you may wish to get help from your auditors in preparing it.

The next step is to develop a list of underwriters who appear to meet the criteria you have set so far (e.g., national or regional, industry specialization). Your auditors, attorneys, and bankers can help you identify those firms and perform a preliminary evaluation of them based on the following:

- **Reputation.** Prospective investors consider the reputation of your managing underwriters—sometimes it even overshadows the merits of the offering itself. A well-respected underwriting firm will be better able to form a strong underwriting syndicate to sell your securities. An underwriter earns its reputation by providing top-quality, reliable service to clients—and will strive to safeguard that reputation by continuing to provide good service.

- **Experience.** Your underwriters should have experience in underwriting initial public offerings and in the type of security you intend to offer (e.g., equity, debt, or a combination). It is beneficial if your underwriters also have experience in your industry as a basis for pricing your stock, and selecting an appropriate underwriting syndicate, as well as providing credibility in the eyes of investors and industry analysts.

- **Syndication and Distribution Capability.** Depending on the size of your offering, the number of geographic markets in which you wish to offer your securities, and the mix of investors you hope to reach (retail or institutional), your managing underwriters may need to establish a syndicate of from 10 to more than 50 underwriters. A broad distribution not only will provide a larger market for your shares, but will help avoid concentration of major blocks of shares in the hands of a few persons. Your underwriters' ability to attract institutional interest in your offering may be a big factor in your success. Most initial public offerings will require participation by institutional investors to generate interest in the volume of shares being offered. Accordingly, your underwriters should have appropriate syndication experience, a broad client base, and a retail and institutional investor orientation consistent with your needs.

- **Aftermarket Support.** An important part of the underwriters' service is to provide aftermarket support for your shares. This is accomplished by having the managing underwriters and some or all of the syndicated underwriters act as market-makers in your shares. Market-makers offer to buy or sell shares at a firm price from the public or in the interdealer market, and generally sustain the financial community's interest in your shares by disseminating information about your company's progress. You can evaluate the underwriters' aftermarket performance by tracking share prices in a number of initial public offerings underwritten by the firm.

Some underwriters also may be prepared to cooperate with your efforts to contact the management of several of the companies they have recently underwritten for a recommendation. Some questions you may wish to ask are:

- Did the underwriters provide all the services they promised to your satisfaction?
- Did the underwriters display an interest in and knowledge of your industry and company, and maintain interest after the initial offering?
- Did the underwriters significantly reduce the stock split ratio or estimated selling price during the registration process?
- Did the underwriters present any last-minute surprises or demands?
- Are you satisfied with the breadth of the underwriting syndicate and placement of your shares?
- What happened to your share price in the aftermarket? To what extent do you believe price movements were related to the appropriateness of the initial offering price, the level of aftermarket support from the underwriters, or other factors?
- Do the managing underwriters continue to promote your company through regular research reports and provide you with other financial advice?
- Would you use the same group to underwrite another offering and recommend them to other companies?
- Is there anything else I should know about this underwriting firm?

Research Capability

A very important component of developing and maintaining market interest is the underwriters' analysis and distribution of information about your company and your industry. Your underwriters' research department should have the resources necessary to produce that information and a reputation that commands the respect of investors—particularly institutional investors—and the financial community in general.

Continuing Financial Advisory Services

The managing underwriters should have the resources to continue to provide your company with investment banking services. This would include assistance in obtaining additional capital as the need arises (whether from private or public sources), advising on proposed mergers or acquisitions, and generally providing a full range of investment banking services.

Cost

While the cost of underwriting is substantial and cannot be ignored, it should be a less important criterion in selecting your underwriters. In the early stages of evaluating prospective underwriters, you will not be able to compare costs, because commissions and other forms of underwriters' compensation are a matter of negotiation.

Once you have formally or informally evaluated a number of underwriters based on the foregoing criteria, you can develop a "short list" of underwriters to approach directly. There are varying opinions as to how many underwriters you should negotiate with at the same time. One school of thought—subscribed to by some underwriters and others—warns against "shopping" for underwriters and recommends approaching only one firm at a time. Another viewpoint holds that some "shopping"—and the resulting competition—would be to your advantage.

How many underwriters you approach will depend partly on the attractiveness of your offering. If the offering is small and highly speculative, the aim may be to find one investment banker willing to underwrite the offering. In a relatively small offering, the underwriter's commission also will be modest. Under these circumstances, underwriters will be less willing to spend a significant amount of time investigating your company and negotiating with you unless they are sure of getting your business.

On the other hand, if your offering is large and likely to be attractive to underwriters, you may be well advised to approach three or four underwriters on a preliminary basis. However, be sure to let them know that you are approaching other underwriters and be candid about every other aspect of your company and the offering as well. If the offering is attractive, underwriters will happily spend the necessary time with you.

Approaching those underwriters on your short list may be handled directly or indirectly through your auditors, attorneys, bankers, or business acquaintances. You also should consider whether you wish to retain more than one managing underwriter. The use of co-managing underwriters, particularly for larger offerings, can be advantageous with respect to initial market coverage, research capabilities, and aftermarket support.

While holding discussions with these underwriters, and in selecting your managing underwriters, bear in mind that you will have a relationship with the individuals assigned to your account. Therefore, you should feel comfortable with them on a personal level.

WORKING WITH YOUR UNDERWRITERS

You will work closely with your managing underwriters in the preparatory stages prior to your public offering, through the completion of your offering, and often long into the future on subsequent public offerings, mergers, or acquisitions.

Underwriters examine a company and its prospects in much the same way that an investor would, but much more intensively. Their examination begins with your business plan. This document either will spark the interest of the underwriters or lead to rejection, so it should be prepared well and present your company in its best light. But here, and in all future dealings with your underwriters, you must scrupulously avoid any mis-representation. If the underwriters find they have been misled, they will abort the offering—leaving you with delays, lost time, and a tarnished reputation.

If the underwriters decide to investigate further, they will delve into various aspects of your business. They will interview key executives, scrutinize your financial statements, challenge your accounting policies, and examine your financial projec-tions. Often they also will meet with your auditors to obtain their views. They will evaluate your products in relation to your industry, talk to your suppliers and customers, as well as assess your market share, technological sophistication, and market growth potential. The intended use of the proceeds of the of-fering also will be taken into consideration. In short, they will perform a thorough evaluation of your company to decide whether or not to handle your offering and, if they are selected, to price and promote your offering.

While we noted earlier that cost is not the most important consideration in selecting your managing underwriters, under-writers come at a high price. Their primary source of compen-sation is a commission, but they will sometimes request other forms of compensation, such as stock options or warrants. The compensation arrangements should be clearly agreed upon be-fore starting with the registration. Some common factors to be considered in negotiating terms with your underwriters are dis-cussed next.

Letter of Intent

The final underwriting agreement is usually not signed until the morning of the day the registration statement is to become effective. Accordingly, there is no legal obligation for either your company or the underwriters to proceed with the offering until that time. Neither underwriters nor companies generally abort a public offering after the registration process has begun except under the most unusual circumstances, and then it is typically by mutual consent (for example, if the "window" has closed for initial public offerings in a particular industry).

Many underwriters will prepare a letter of intent that is signed by the managing underwriters and your company management. The letter of intent often details the agreed-upon underwriters' commission, estimated offering price, and other negotiated terms, but does not create a legal obligation for either your company or the underwriters to proceed with the offering. The letter may, however, create a binding obligation for the company to pay certain expenses incurred if the offering is not completed.

Types of Underwriting

There are two common types of underwriting agreements: "firm commitment" and "best efforts." In a "firm commitment" underwriting agreement, the underwriters agree to purchase all the shares in the offering and then resell them to the public. Any shares not sold to the public are paid for and held by the underwriters for their own account. This type of agreement provides you with the most assurance of raising the required funds and is used by most of the larger underwriters.

Often the underwriters also are given an "overallotment option" that allows them to purchase up to a specific number of additional shares from the company in the event the underwriters sell more shares than the underwriting agreement stipulates. Overallotment options take various forms. In some situations, the company will issue additional shares if the option is exercised, while in others the additional shares will be provided from holdings of existing shareholders. The existence of an overallotment option (or "green shoe" option, named after the Green Shoe Manufacturing Company, which introduced this technique) must be disclosed in the prospectus.

In a "best efforts" underwriting agreement, the underwriters simply agree to use their best efforts to sell the shares on behalf of your company. Some "best efforts" are all-or-nothing arrangements in which the offering is withdrawn if the shares cannot all be sold. Others set a lower minimum number of shares that must be sold for the offering to be completed.

The obvious drawback of a "best efforts" underwriting arrangement is that you are not assured of obtaining the required amounts of capital. You may receive insufficient capital for your needs but still have to assume the responsibilities of being a public company.

Offering Price

Underwriters generally will not and cannot guarantee an offering price (or, in the case of debt securities, an interest rate) and total proceeds in advance. The offering price is not finalized until just before the registration statement becomes effective because it must be responsive to current market conditions. If the underwriters are unwilling to predict an offering price, as is true for many underwriters, they will generally estimate a range for the offering price based on existing market conditions at the time of their estimate. While such estimates are in no way binding and will change in response to changing market conditions up to the effective date of the offering, they will reduce the chance of misunderstandings and last-minute surprises.

Underwriting Commission

The underwriting commission, or discount, is generally the single largest expense in a public offering. For recent initial public offerings, the rate of commission has generally been in the range of 6 percent to 10 percent. Debt offerings generally result in lower rates of commission than do common stock offerings. In determining the rate of commission to charge, underwriters consider a number of factors that affect how much effort they will have to expend in selling your shares. These factors include the size of the offering, competitive rates for offerings of similar size, the type of underwriting (i.e., "firm commitment" or "best efforts"), and the marketability of the shares. There may also be a trade-off between the rate of commission and other forms of compensation, particularly for smaller offerings, as discussed next.

Underwriter Warrants

Some underwriters will negotiate for stock warrants in addition to their commission. Such warrants are more common when dealing with smaller underwriters and smaller offerings. If granting stock warrants can be traded off for a lower commission rate, the obvious advantage is increased net proceeds from the offering, although some dilution of shareholders' equity will result. Be sure to reach agreement on the number and terms of the warrants in advance to avoid last-minute misunderstandings.

Reimbursement of Underwriters' Expenses

It is common, particularly for smaller offerings, for the managing underwriters to request reimbursement for some of their expenses incurred for your offering. For example, legal fees incurred by the underwriters' review for compliance with state securities laws are often reimbursed by the issuer. These legal fees will increase with the number of states in which you offer your shares, as a result of each state's filing requirements. You may therefore wish to discuss the area of geographic syndication in the negotiations stage, before the underwriting syndicate is established by your managing underwriters. You may also be able to negotiate a limit to the amount of underwriters' expenses you will be required to reimburse.

Rights of First Refusal

Some underwriters will request a right of first refusal on any future underwritings by your company. While such a request may seem innocuous, it can adversely affect future offerings. Other underwriters will be reluctant to invest the time and resources necessary to evaluate a proposed offering if they know they may be preempted by another underwriter's right of first refusal. If a right of first refusal cannot be avoided, you should consider negotiating either a time limit after which the right expires or a provision that the right expires any time it is available but not exercised.

PRICING YOUR STOCK

Determining an appropriate offering price for your securities is one of the most difficult decisions you and your underwriters will have to make. But even before tackling that decision, you must decide on what type of security to offer.

Most initial public offerings consist of common stock, while some consist of units that include both common stock and warrants to purchase additional shares of common stock. There are other possibilities such as debt, preferred stock, or units that include common stock and convertible debentures. Generally it is not practicable to issue only convertible securities in the absence of an established public market for the common stock that would be obtained on conversion. Some of the factors to consider in determining how to structure your offering include:

- The cash flow consequences of interest and dividend requirements for debt and preferred stock, respectively;
- Resulting debt-to-equity ratio;
- The potential dilution introduced by stock warrants; and
- The income tax implications.

The final pricing decision is not made until just before the underwriting agreement is signed—generally the day before or the morning of the effective date of the registration statement. But the background research, comparisons, analysis, and discussions will have begun well in advance of that date.

Offering prices of shares of common stock are often referred to and compared on the basis of price-earnings ratios—one of the most important considerations in comparing a proposed price to other current public offerings or existing public companies in your industry. A variety of other factors also are considered. The projected impact on earnings resulting from the proposed use of the new funds, past and projected rate of growth, and the quality of past earnings (e.g., whether they include extraordinary or nonrecurring gains or losses) will all affect the price of your shares. Another factor is the dilution issue—the possibility of decreased ownership if other shareholders are given an opportunity to exercise outstanding warrants. Your company's vulnerability to competition, relative management strength, planned acquisitions, size of the offering, and location in a "glamour industry" also will come into play.

In short, pricing your stock is more of an art than a science, and your underwriters' experience enables them to advise you on an appropriate price. Although it is tempting to set as high a price as possible—particularly if a secondary offering of existing shareholders' stock is included—overpricing should be avoided. Underwriters typically advise a company to set a price that will produce an active aftermarket in the shares. Overpricing tends to destroy investor confidence, possibly creating a downward spiral in share price. By pricing to allow for a modest price rise in the immediate aftermarket, you can stimulate public interest.

Some new issues realize substantial price increases in the early weeks of the aftermarket, leading some to conclude that the offering price was seriously understated. In most cases, however, the price increase is more reflective of undue public optimism than underwriting error, and within a relatively short time the stock price generally returns to the more realistic levels anticipated by the underwriter.

Finally, you must decide on the number of shares to be offered. To support active trading in the aftermarket, most underwriters believe a minimum of from 800 thousand to 1 million shares is necessary for a sufficiently broad distribution. But because the number of shares offered and the offering price are directly related, many companies are advised to split their stock to establish an appropriate number of shares for the offering.

Stock splits also are often motivated by a need to bring the of-fering price within an acceptable range. Many consider this range to be between $5 and $20 per share, depending on the industry (although many "high-risk" offerings are made at $1 or less per share). These stock splits do not affect the price-earnings multiple.

5

THE REGISTRATION PROCESS

The registration process begins, for the SEC's purposes, when you have reached a preliminary understanding with an underwriter on your proposed public offering. From that point on, you become subject to SEC regulations (which are discussed later in this chapter) on what you may and may not do to promote your company. The heart of the registration process, however, is the preparation and review of the registration statement, and registration is ultimately affected by the filing of a final registration statement with the SEC.

PREPARING YOUR REGISTRATION STATEMENT

The registration statement consists of two parts: Part I is the prospectus which is widely distributed to underwriters and prospective investors. Part II contains additional information which is required by, and provided to, the SEC. The entire registration statement becomes part of the public record and is available for public inspection.

The SEC has established the informational content, as well as a generally standardized sequence and form for registration statements. Information requirements vary depending on the nature of the securities being registered, the size of the offering, the type of organization issuing the securities and its industry, and the length of time the company has been an SEC registrant.

Various registration forms are specified or allowed in different circumstances. For example, "seasoned" public companies that have been subject to the SEC periodic reporting requirements for three or more years may, in certain circumstances, use abbreviated registration forms (S-2 or S-3) that incorporate certain information by reference from their periodic reports filed with the SEC (10-Q or 10-QSB, 10-K or 10-KSB and 8-K) as well as proxy statements sent to shareholders. Other forms are specified for use by real estate companies; by investment companies and trusts; for registering securities issued in connection with reorganizations, mergers, and acquisitions; for registering securities offered to employees under stock option and other benefit plans; and in various other circumstances.

Form S-1 is the registration form most commonly used in initial public offerings for larger companies. Form S-1 imposes no limitation on the amount of funds that can be raised.

Regulation S-B makes it easier for small businesses to raise money in the capital markets. The rules simplify the initial and ongoing disclosure and filing requirements for qualifying small businesses and broaden the limits of existing rules relating to small offerings. To file a registration statement under Regulation S-B, your company must meet the definition of a small business issuer as discussed in Chapter 8. Regulation S-B includes two new registration statements for eligible small business issuers: Forms SB-1 and SB-2. Form SB-2 imposes no limit on the amount of funds that can be raised; however, Form SB-1 establishes a limit of $10 million in any 12-month period. While Form SB-2 does not impose any limits on the amount of funds that can be raised, this form generally is not used for equity offerings of $25 million or more because the company could not qualify as a small business issuer in the future.

A registration statement usually requires a considerable period of time to prepare. The statement must contain all disclosures, both favorable and unfavorable, necessary to enable investors to make well-informed decisions, and the document must not include any materially misleading statements.

Exhibit 5–1 summarizes the information required in Form S-1. (Appendix E contains a more detailed discussion of the information required in Forms S-1 and SB-2.) Item 11, "Information with respect to registrant," is the most time-consuming and difficult item to prepare. Item 11 contains the requirements for (1) information about the company's business, properties, and management; (2) financial statements and other

---

EXHIBIT 5–1.   Form S-1 Information Requirements.

Part 1: Information Required in Prospectus

Item

1. Forepart of registration statement and outside front cover page of prospectus
2. Inside front and outside back cover pages of prospectus
3. Summary information, risk factors, and ratio of earnings to fixed charges*
4. Use of proceeds
5. Determination of offering price
6. Dilution
7. Selling security holders
8. Plan of distribution
9. Description of securities to be registered
10. Interests of named experts and counsel
11. Information with respect to registrant
12. Disclosure of Commission position on indemnification for Securities Act liabilities

Part 2: Information Not Required in Prospectus

Item

13. Other expenses of issuance and distribution
14. Indemnification of directors and officers
15. Recent sales of unregistered securities
16. Exhibits and financial statement schedules
17. Undertakings

---

* The ratio of earnings to fixed charges is not required in equity offerings. See the Glossary for a definition of the ratio of earnings to fixed charges.

financial information; and (3) management's discussion and analysis of financial condition and results of operations.

The contents of the registration statement, including the financial statements and other information in the prospectus, are detailed in various SEC rules and regulations:

- Regulation S-X governs the form and content of financial statements (except for small business issuers).

- Regulation S-K governs disclosures not related to the financial statements (except for small business issuers).

- Financial Reporting Releases (FRRs) interpret certain of the financial statement requirements of Regulation S-X and other accounting practices. They have the status of a regulation.

- Staff Accounting Bulletins (SABs) are published interpretations and practices followed by the SEC staff.

- Regulation S-B governs for eligible small business issuers the form, content, and periods to be covered in financial statements, as well as disclosures not related to the financial statements.

- Regulation C prescribes the procedures to be followed in preparing and filing a registration statement (e.g., paper size, numbers of copies).

These SEC requirements are highly technical and ever-changing, so most companies rely on their auditors and attorneys to help them interpret and apply the requirements.

The first step in preparing the registration statement is the initial "all-hands" meeting, including company executives, attorneys, auditors, underwriters, and underwriters' attorneys. At this meeting, responsibility for gathering information and preparing various parts of the registration statement is assigned. Typically, the attorneys play a coordinating role in directing this team effort, and the parties agree on deadlines for providing the required information and drafts to the attorneys.

The entire registration team ordinarily participates in the initial drafting of the registration statement. The company and its legal counsel generally prepare the nonfinancial sections (if the company's legal counsel is inexperienced in preparing registration statements, the underwriters' counsel assists). The managing underwriter and underwriters' counsel prepare the description of the offering. The company prepares the required financial statements and schedules, as well as other financial disclosures. The independent accountant usually advises the company about the financial statements and disclosures.

As the various sections of the registration statement are assimilated, disclosures are reviewed, considered, and often redrafted. Two purposes of the prospectus, often viewed as conflicting, will become evident at this stage.

First, the prospectus is used as a selling document by your managing underwriters in forming an underwriting syndicate, and by the syndicate to sell your securities. Therefore, you will want to present your company and the offering in the best possible light.

Second, the prospectus, as a disclosure document, serves in accordance with the 1933 Act as protection against any liability for misleading and omitted material information on the part of controlling shareholders, executives, directors, underwriters, and experts providing information for the registration statement. As a result, all concerned will want to stress that all negative factors or investor "risk factors" related to your offering and your company are given at least equal prominence with the positive factors.

Balancing these conflicting purposes draws on the experience of your attorneys, auditors, and underwriters. While the final document may not paint as bright a picture as you may have preferred, or indeed considered appropriate, rest assured that underwriters and investors are accustomed to, and thus discount, the tone found in all prospectuses and are adept at extracting the salient factors in the document.

Following the initial meeting, the offering timetable and a letter of intent between the company and the lead underwriter should be formalized. The timetable should detail the tasks to be performed, the identity of those responsible for each, and the completion date of each task. (See Exhibit 5–2 for a sample timetable.) The nonbinding letter of intent confirms the intended nature of the underwriting (i.e., "best efforts" or "firm commitment"), the underwriters' compensation, the number of shares expected to be issued, and the anticipated price. A binding underwriting agreement is not signed until the registration statement is about to become effective.

Due Diligence

"Due diligence" is a term you will hear often during the registration process. As the term implies, it relates to a reasonable investigation that will support your belief that the statements made in the registration statement are true and do not omit any information necessary to make them not misleading. The exercise of due diligence with respect to any particular statement or disclosure will imply differing responsibilities, depending on the position and role of the individual and the nature of the information.

EXHIBIT 5–2. Example Timetable for an Initial Public Offering.

Day	Activity
1	First "All-Hands" meeting
45	First draft of Registration Statement
50	Second meeting—Revisions agreed upon
55	Third meeting
60	File Registration Statement with the SEC
70–100	"Road Show"
90	Receive SEC comment letter
90–110	Revisions and pricing
115	Effective date
120	Closing

Under the 1933 Act, a company is absolutely liable, regardless of due diligence, for any material misstatements or omissions in its registration statement. However, the directors, controlling shareholders, underwriters, experts, corporate officers, and others who sign the registration statement may claim a due diligence defense if such deficiencies come to light.

Certain common due diligence procedures have evolved over time and in response to various court cases. For example, the courts have held that you and the others involved in the registration statement cannot assign responsibility for a due diligence entirely to your attorneys or to some other person. This does not mean, however, that every individual must personally verify each statement or disclosure made in the prospectus. You may, for example, rely on statements made by your independent auditors and other experts as long as you have no reason not to believe those statements.

At a minimum, each person involved in preparing the registration statement should read it in its entirety. You can also expect your attorneys and your underwriters' attorneys to probe deeply into your company and its affairs in carrying out their due diligence procedures. Your company's officers and directors should answer candidly any questions about the company and statements made in the prospectus about the firm and its offering. The questions will delve into management's experience, compensation arrangements, and their contracts or transactions with the company.

In carrying out their due diligence procedures, your underwriters typically ask your auditors to supply a "comfort letter" detailing the specific procedures they have carried out with respect to the unaudited financial data contained in the registration statement. The letter may provide "negative assurance"—a statement that nothing came to the auditors' attention which indicated that the unaudited financial statements and other financial data were not prepared in accordance with GAAP applied on a consistent basis. Generally, the letter is dated both as of the effective date and as of the closing date, or a separate letter is issued on each of those dates. A draft of such a letter typically is provided to the underwriters in advance to obtain preliminary agreement from all parties on the specified procedures.

Finally, a due diligence conference is generally held shortly before the effective date. This meeting brings together your managing underwriters and the underwriting syndicate, your company's chief executive officer, financial executives, attorneys, auditors, and the underwriters' attorneys. This meeting is held primarily to give members of the underwriting syndicate an opportunity to raise any "last minute" questions about the offering and your company. Questions at this meeting principally will focus on events or financial performance of the company that have occurred since the registration statement was initially drafted. If significant events have occurred that would be important to investors, the registration statement should be revised to discuss such developments.

CONTENT OF A REGISTRATION STATEMENT

Most initial public offerings are filed on Form S-1. Although registration statements are referred to by form numbers, they are prepared in a narrative and reasonably flexible format. The SEC requires certain minimum disclosures, and a standardized sequence and style has evolved over time. Nevertheless, a significant degree of judgment is required in drafting these disclosures.

Part I—Prospectus

The following is a summary of the major items generally required in Part I of the registration statement, the prospectus:

- **Outside Front Cover.** Shows key facts about the offering, including the name of the company; the title, amount, and a brief description of the securities offered; a table showing the offering price, underwriting discounts and commissions, proceeds to the company; and the date of the prospectus. If the offering is a secondary or partial secondary offering, a statement to that effect is included, and the proceeds to selling shareholders are shown. Generally, the managing underwriters' name is shown as well.

- **Inside Front and Outside Back Cover.** Includes a table of contents, information about price stabilization, and a statement on dealers' delivery requirements for the prospectus.

- **Prospectus Summary.** May include an overview of the company and its business, a brief description of the security offered, estimated net proceeds and use of those proceeds, and selected financial data.

- **The Company.** Provides more detailed background information on the company, including where and when it was incorporated, location of its principal offices, and a brief description of its primary business activities.

- **Risk Factors.** Highlights any factors that make the offering risky or speculative. Examples include dependence on a single supplier or a few customers, existing contractual restrictions on the company, an unproven market for your product, lack of business experience or earnings history, existence of plans put in place by the Company to deter unwanted takeovers, material dilution to public investors as a result of the offering, or potential dilution that may result from the exercise of any outstanding stock options or warrants. For particularly speculative offerings, this section must also be referenced on the prospectus cover.

- **Use of Proceeds.** Discloses the principal intended use of the net proceeds of the offering, including specified details if the offering is to reduce debt or acquire a new business. If there is no specific plan for the proceeds, the reason for the offering must be disclosed.

- **Dilution.** Describes, generally in tabular form, any material dilution of the prospective purchasers' equity interest caused by a disparity between the public offering price and tangible book value of the shares immediately preceding the offering. Because existing shareholders often will have acquired their shares at a significantly lower cost than the offering price (e.g., company founders, or through employee stock option or award plans), material dilution often does occur for new purchasers.

- **Dividend Policy.** Discloses the company's dividend history and present dividend policy. Any restrictions on the payment of dividends also must be disclosed. If a determination has been made to reinvest future earnings instead of paying dividends, as many newly public companies do, that fact also is disclosed.

- **Capitalization.** Discloses the company's debt and equity capital structure, both before and after the offering. The "pro forma" capital structure after the offering is adjusted to reflect the securities issued and the intended use of the proceeds (e.g., to reduce long-term debt).

- **Selected Financial Data.** Summarizes financial information for each of the last five years, and usually for the interim period since the last year-end and the comparative interim period of the preceding year. This data generally includes net sales or operating revenue; income (or loss) from continuing operations, both in total and per share amounts; total assets; long-term debt; capital leases; redeemable preferred stock; and cash dividends per share. Companies may include additional data that would enhance an understanding of, and would highlight trends in, their financial condition and results of operations. As more fully explained in Chapter 8, small business issuers filing on Forms SB-1 or SB-2 are not required to furnish selected financial data.

- **Management's Discussion and Analysis.** MD&A answers the question "why" for the financial condition and results of operations presented in the financial statements, the purpose of which is to provide investors with both past and forward-looking information and management's assessments of past and prospective performance.

MD&A disclosures are particularly important in an initial public offering registration statement. The SEC staff usually reviews the section thoroughly and often makes numerous comments. The specific requirements for MD&A are set forth in Item 303 of Regulation S-K and in FRR 36, an interpretive release that provides further guidance to registrants in their preparation of MD&A. The SEC believes registrants should be guided by the general purpose of the MD&A requirements, "to give investors an opportunity to look at the registrant through the eyes of management by providing an historical and prospective analysis of the registrant's financial condition and results of operations, with particular emphasis on the registrant's prospects for the future."

Since the release of FRR 36, the SEC has continued to monitor the adequacy of registrant disclosures through its reviews of MD&A and in 1992 issued its first enforcement action against a registrant (Caterpillar, Inc.) solely for inadequate disclosure in MD&A.* The SEC reviews previously filed documents, with the benefit of hindsight, to see if material events disclosed in a current report were appropriately disclosed in previous MD&A.

- **Overview.** Management must discuss the registrant's results of operations, liquidity, and capital resources. The discussion generally should cover the same period covered by the financial statements. The instructions suggest traditional year-to-year comparisons (e.g., 19X5 vs. 19X4 and 19X4 vs. 19X3), but other formats may be used if the registrant

---

*Other MD&A enforcement actions followed: In 1994 America West Airlines, Inc. and Salant Corporation were cited for failure to disclose liquidity uncertainties in MD&A. Shared Medical Systems, Inc. was also cited in 1994 for failure to disclose known, material trends in sales.

believes they would aid reader understanding. When trend information is relevant, it may be necessary for the discussion to refer to the five-year table of selected financial data. The SEC suggested in FRR 36 that management use the statement of cash flows for a source of MD&A discussions of liquidity and capital resources. This generally produces discussion more comparable from registrant to registrant.

- **Liquidity.** Regulation S-K defines liquidity as the registrant's ability to generate adequate amounts of cash to meet both current and future needs. Many accountants interpret "needs" as encompassing the registrant's need to pay obligations as they mature, to maintain capacity, to provide for planned growth, and to provide a competitive return on investment. The registrant must examine its individual circumstances and identify those balance sheet, income, and cash flow items that indicate its liquidity.

  The SEC wants management to explain the considerations it views as important to the registrant's liquidity. The requirements do not specify any particular financial statement conditions or items that must be discussed, but FRR 36 suggests the use of the statement of cash flows. The instructions call for the subject of liquidity to be discussed within the context of the registrant's own business, on both a short- and long-term basis. In that regard, the SEC in FRR 36 reminds management to look beyond the next 12-month period.

  Companies also need to disclose information about anticipated cash resources and requirements, significant restrictions and covenants stipulated by debt agreements, account balance and average interest rates on short-term borrowings, instances where cash outlays for income taxes materially exceed income tax expense, and other liquidity information.

- **Capital Resources.** Regulation S-K does not define the term "capital resources," but mentions equity, debt, and off-balance sheet financing arrangements as examples.

Disclosure should include a discussion of material commitments for capital expenditures, their purpose, as well as any material trends in the registrant's capital resources. Such disclosures should be quantified to the extent practical.

In addition, companies that disclose plans for future expansion or other anticipated capital expenditure requirements should discuss prospective information regarding sources of capital to fund the planned expansion. Again, the SEC also reminds management to look beyond the next 12-month period.

The discussion of capital resources and liquidity are closely related. Many registrants choose to discuss the two in combination in MD&A.

- **Results of Operations.** In discussing the results of operations, management should:

  — Describe any unusual or infrequent events or transactions or any significant economic changes that materially affect income from continuing operations, and the extent to which income was affected. Examples of such transactions include the sale of assets or operations, early debt refunding, and LIFO inventory liquidations. It is not necessary to repeat the disclosures of items in the financial statements, but registrants should address the impact of these transactions on cash flow and reported profits and trends, the estimated effect on future operations, and whether it was a "one time" transaction.

  — Describe any other significant components of revenue or expense necessary to understand the results of operations.

  — Describe any known trends or uncertainties that have had, or are expected to have, a material impact on sales, revenue, or income from continuing operations.

  — Disclose any future changes in the relationship between costs and revenue if events are known that will cause a material change, such as known future increases in labor or materials costs or prices.

— Discuss the extent to which material increases in net sales or revenue are due to increased sales volume, introduction of new products or services, or increased sales prices.

- **Description of Business.** Provides investors with detailed insight into your company's business operations. Items addressed in this section include:

— General development of the company and the business during the last five years.

— Future operating plans if the company has not had revenue from operations in each of the last three years.

— For each major geographic area: revenue, operating profit or loss, assets, and export sales for each of the last three years.

— For each major industry segment: revenue, operating profit or loss, and assets for each of the last three years. (Some of the information below is also presented by industry segment.)

These disclosures should be consistent with those provided in the audited financial statements.

— Principal products or services and their markets.

— Status of any publicly announced new products or business segments.

— Sources and availability of raw materials.

— Any patents, trademarks, licenses, franchises, and concessions held.

— Extent to which business is or may be seasonal.

— Practices with respect to working capital items—for example, if required to carry significant amounts of inventory to meet rapid customer delivery requirements.

— Any significant dependence on a single or a few customers.

— Amount of any firm backlog of orders.

— Government contracts potentially subject to termination or renegotiation.

— Competitive conditions.

— Expenditures for research and development in each of the last three years.

— Effects of environmental laws.

— Number of employees.

- **Properties.** Discloses the location and a brief description of the major plants, mines, and other important physical properties owned or leased.

- **Legal Proceedings.** Describes any material pending legal proceedings, other than ordinary routine litigation incidental to the business.

- **Management and Certain Security Holders.** Provides certain key information on the business experience and compensation of management, and on major shareholders. These disclosure requirements often give rise to objections from management because they now must publicly disclose the following information, much of which is generally considered strictly confidential by a private company:

  — The names, ages, and business experience (and any involvement in specified legal proceedings) of all current or nominated directors and executive officers and other key employees.

  — The compensation, both direct and indirect (including stock options and other benefits), current and proposed, for directors and certain executives.

  — Loans to management and directors (and their immediate families) and certain transactions with management, directors, and major shareholders (and their immediate families).

— Transactions with promoters, if the company has been in existence for less than five years.

— Certain compensatory arrangements with officers and directors contingent on their resignation or termination or on a change in control of the company (known as "golden parachute" arrangements).

— The share holdings of all officers and directors, and of those shareholders who beneficially own more than 5 percent of any class of shares.

- **Description of Securities to Be Registered.** Describes the particular securities being offered, including the title of the security, dividend rights, conversion and voting rights, and liquidation rights. The terms of any warrants or rights offered also are described.

- **Underwriting.** Describes the underwriting and plan of distribution for the securities offered, including the names of the principal underwriters in the syndicate, the number of shares underwritten by each underwriter, the method of underwriting, and any material relationships between the company and any of those underwriters. The underwriters' compensation, board representation, and indemnification also are disclosed.

- **Legal Matters, Experts, and Additional Information.** Briefly identifies the attorneys and their opinion on the validity of the securities offered (and discloses any shareholdings in the company held by the attorneys), identifies any experts who have been relied on in the preparation of the registration statement, and refers to the availability of additional information in Part II of the registration statement filed with the SEC.

- **Changes in and Disagreements with Independent Auditors.** Discloses circumstances surrounding changes in auditors during the past two fiscal years, including whether there were any disagreements between management and the former auditors or other reportable events on accounting, auditing, or financial reporting matters. Disclosure also is required of certain consultations between management and the current auditors that occurred before the change in auditors.

- **Financial Statements.** Contains the financial statements, including the auditors' report, for the following periods:
  - Audited balance sheets as of the end of each of the last two fiscal years (one year for small business issuers under Regulation S-B).
  - Audited statements of income, cash flows, and shareholders' equity for each of the last three fiscal years (two years for small business issuers under Regulation S-B).
  - If the anticipated effective date of the registration statement is more than 134 days after your fiscal year-end, unaudited interim statements must be provided, with comparative unaudited interim statements (statements of income and cash flows) for the preceding year. Exhibit 5–3 shows the latest financial statements required under various circumstances in an initial public offering for a company with a December 31 year-end.
  - Financial statements included in SEC filings generally must be consolidated, subject to certain narrowly defined exceptions relating, for example, to certain subsidiaries in which control is likely to be temporary or does not rest with the majority owner. Subsidiaries should be consolidated unless this would not result in the most meaningful and useful disclosure.*
  - The SEC requires that separate financial statements be presented for unconsolidated subsidiaries and

---

*The SEC Staff indicated in SAB 93 (Topic 5:Z) that the expected change in control must be outside of the control of the registrant in order to rely on this exception to consolidation requirements.

EXHIBIT 5–3. Form S-1 Financial Statement Requirements.

Expected effective date	January 1, 19X2 to February 14, 19X2	February 15, 19X2 to May 14, 19X2[e]	May 15, 19X2[e] to December 31, 19X2
The most recent audited financial statements must be as of a date no earlier than[a]	December 31, 19X0[b]	December 31, 19X1	December 31, 19X1
The most recent condensed unaudited interim financial statements must be as of a date no earlier than[c]	September 30, 19X1	None	[d]

[a] If the annual audited financial statements included in the registration statement are "not recent" (e.g., nine months old at the effective date), underwriters often require audited interim financial statements as of a more recent date.

[b] Unless more recent audited financial statements are available.

[c] In addition to the condensed unaudited interim financial statements, financial information describing the results of subsequent months may be necessary to prevent the registration statement from being misleading (e.g., if the company incurs operating losses or develops severe liquidity problems).

[d] Filings made 134 days after the company's fiscal year-end must include a balance sheet as of an interim date within 135 days of the date of filing.

[e] Does not consider the effects on the financial statements requirements of a leap year.

investees that individually are greater than 20 percent of consolidated assets or income for the latest year. Also, if the 20 percent threshold is not met but unconsolidated subsidiaries and investees aggregate more than 10 percent of consolidated assets or income, summarized financial information or separate financial statements must be presented. Small business issuers filing under Regulation S-B need only provide summarized financial information for individual unconsolidated subsidiaries or investees that exceed 20 percent of consolidated assets or income.

— Separate audited financial statements also are required for certain businesses that recently have been or probably will be acquired. Depending on how significant the acquired business is to the consolidated statements, the periods required to be presented vary from one to three years. Separate financial statements are required only for those periods prior to the acquisition.

— Pro forma financial information also may be required in certain circumstances. Pro forma financial information is historical information adjusted "as if" a given transaction had occurred at an earlier time. It generally includes a condensed income statement for the latest year and any subsequent interim period, and a condensed balance sheet as of the end of the latest period presented. Pro forma information generally must be provided for significant business acquisitions and dispositions, reorganizations, unusual asset exchanges, and debt restructurings.

— In addition to the information specifically required, the SEC staff will request, and prudence dictates, the disclosure of any other material information. An omitted fact is material if there is a substantial likelihood that a reasonable investor would consider it important in deciding whether to buy the security at the price offered.

Part II

The second part of the registration statement does not form part of the printed prospectus provided to the investing public. However, this information is filed with the SEC and becomes available for public inspection. The following information is typically provided in Part II:

- Summary of expenses incurred by the company in connection with the issuance and distribution of the securities.
- Indemnification or insurance for liability of directors and officers acting for the company.
- Sales of unregistered securities in the last three years.
- Various financial statement schedules. This requirement is not applicable for small business issuers under Regulation S-B.
- Various exhibits, including a list of all subsidiaries, the underwriting agreement, the corporate charter and bylaws, and any material contracts.
- Written consent of all experts who have prepared or certified any of the material included in the registration statement.

Preparation Procedures

After the registration statement has been drafted and circulated to the registration team, a joint meeting of all drafting parties is held to review and comment on it. The draft is modified as appropriate (several redrafts may be necessary), and the amended copy is sent to the printer for the first proof. The printer's proof goes through the same circulation, comment, and revision process. When the registration team is satisfied with the document, it is distributed to the board of directors for review and approval prior to filing with the SEC and the appropriate state agencies.

Preparing a registration statement that is acceptable to all the parties is extremely difficult and often involves a series of compromises. For example, underwriters' counsel may insist on disclosures about the company that management is initially reluctant to make. These discussions, when coupled with severe time pressures and changing market conditions, can result in frazzled nerves and frayed tempers, particularly as the proposed offering date approaches.

FILING THE INITIAL REGISTRATION STATEMENT AND THE INITIAL REGULATORY REVIEW

When the registration statement has been drafted, but before it is initially filed with the SEC, some companies take advantage of the SEC's willingness to hold a prefiling conference with a registrant or its representatives. These conferences give companies a chance to discuss any important accounting or disclosure matters in advance, minimizing the number of costly and time-consuming revisions that may be necessitated by the SEC's formal review.

Companies should consider the following when planning a meeting with the SEC staff:

- The company's officers should be prepared to explain and support the company's position, as the SEC staff prefers to hear the company's position directly. This also ensures that the company's position is stated correctly and appropriate in the specific circumstances. The company's independent accountants should accompany the officers in this meeting. The company's legal counsel also may attend and, on occasion, consideration should be given to asking the underwriter's representatives to attend.
- Before attending a conference with the SEC staff, necessary documentation should be accumulated. This includes drafts of financial statements, summaries of important questions, and statements of the company's positions. Often a conference can be much more productive if material is sent to the staff for consideration before the conference is held.

- The company should document all communications with the SEC staff that are not written (i.e., telephone calls and meetings, with a memorandum).

It may be desirable for the registrant to send a letter to the SEC staff summarizing the subjects discussed at a prefiling conference and setting forth their understanding of the conclusions reached on accounting matters. This is particularly the case for complex issues where it is important to ensure that all parties clearly understand the conclusions reached. The person addressed is requested to review the letter and advise the registrant if the SEC staff has any comments. Such a letter serves to minimize future differences of opinion as to the conclusions reached. It is not customary to write the SEC staff to confirm a phone discussion; however, this may be desirable in some cases.

When outstanding issues have been resolved to the satisfaction of all concerned and the registration statement has been signed by specified company officers and a majority of the board of directors, it is filed with the SEC together with a transmittal letter and filing fee. At this stage, the registration statement is incomplete only with respect to certain information that is not finalized until the day before, or the morning of, the effective date. This information includes the price and related terms at which the securities will be offered, the underwriting syndicate, the underwriters' and dealers' commissions, and the net proceeds.

The SEC and the states have concurrent jurisdiction over securities offerings. The registration statement must be filed with the SEC, with any state in which the securities will be offered, and with the National Association of Securities Dealers (NASD). The SEC review is designed only to assess compliance with its requirements, including the adequacy of disclosures about the company, without addressing the merits of the offering. In addition to reviewing the adequacy of the disclosures, some states also consider the merits of the offering under their "blue sky" laws (i.e., whether the offering is "fair, just, and equitable") which are discussed later in this chapter. Some states perform in-depth reviews, while others perform cursory reviews. The primary purpose of the NASD's review is to determine whether the underwriters' compensation is excessive.

Based on the reviews, the SEC staff (and sometimes one or more of the states) will issue a formal comment letter. The SEC staff's letter describes the ways in which it believes the filing does not comply with its requirements. The comment letters often focus on the specific uses of the proceeds (including the adequacy of the proceeds for the designated purposes), MD&A of financial condition and results of operations, and disclosures about risk. Comments on the financial statements may question such matters as accounting policies and practices, related-party transactions, unusual compensation arrangements, off-balance-sheet financing methods, or the relationship among certain components of the financial statements.

Copies of the preliminary prospectus, known as a "red herring," are provided to the underwriting syndicate for distribution to prospective investors. It is referred to as a red herring because it must include the following statement on the front cover, printed in red ink:

> *Information contained herein is subject to completion or amendment. A registration statement relating to these securities has been filed with the SEC. These securities may not be sold nor may offers to buy be accepted prior to the time the registration statement becomes effective. This prospectus shall not constitute an offer to sell or the solicitation of an offer to buy nor shall there be any sale of these securities in any State in which such offer, solicitation or sale would be unlawful prior to registration or qualification under the securities laws of any such State.*

Although "red herrings" may be distributed once the initial registration statement is filed, many companies wait until the SEC staff's first round of comments have been cleared before they distribute the documents. This delay is based on a desire to avoid redistributing a revised "red herring" which may have a negative effect on investors' perceptions of the company. This preliminary prospectus does not include a specific final offering price, but discloses a range for it.

The SEC's Division of Corporation Finance reviews registration statements for adequacy of disclosure in accordance with the SEC's regulations and other pronouncements. While the division employs varying levels of review intensity, initial public offerings receive a thorough review by the division's staff, including reviews by an accountant and either an attorney or a financial analyst.

As noted earlier, the purpose of the SEC's review is not to evaluate the quality of an offering, but rather to ensure that you have complied with the relevant form and regulations and have made adequate disclosures. The SEC staff may require you to provide certain disclosures of adverse business conditions or other weaknesses in the offering more prominence, either by cross-referencing to the cover page, by supplying more information, or simply by moving the relevant disclosures closer to the front of the prospectus. They may ask you to support certain claims or statements made in the prospectus—and to remove them if they consider the support inadequate. They also may take issue with a particular choice of accounting policy or may request additional disclosures in the financial statements.

The experience of your professional advisors in identifying those sensitive areas and anticipating potential problems should minimize the number of comments received. However, rarely do first-time registration statements complete the review process without any SEC staff comments.

Your attorneys or auditors will help you address and rectify the deficiencies noted. If the required changes are significant, you may be required to file an amendment with the SEC, and to reprint and redistribute your revised preliminary prospectus to all underwriters. If the SEC staff or your attorneys feel the changes are so material that they must also be brought to the attention of public investors who received the preliminary prospectus, a full recirculation to all investors may be required, increasing your printing costs. If the changes required are less significant, you may be able to send the SEC staff a letter outlining the proposed changes or a printer's proof of the final prospectus showing the proposed changes. You can generally agree on any minor changes by telephone.

Finally, when all deficiencies have been dealt with to the satisfaction of the SEC staff, and your company and professional advisors are satisfied that there have not been any additional material developments in the period since the registration statement was filed, you can ask the SEC staff to declare the registration statement effective.

WHILE YOU WAIT TO "GO EFFECTIVE"

A number of activities begin once your registration statement is initially filed with the SEC. The preliminary prospectus, or "red herring," is used by your managing underwriters to form an underwriting syndicate. Subject to the SEC restrictions on the selling efforts to be used, you and the underwriting syndicate then begin to deal with prospective investors interested in your offering. Finally, just before the effective date of the registration statement, the underwriting agreement is signed.

Underwriters' Syndication

As soon as the preliminary prospectus is filed with the SEC, your managing underwriters begin their efforts to assemble an underwriting syndicate to sell your securities. They will invite various firms to join the syndicate based on your particular offering and the objectives established for it. Depending on the size of the offering, the syndicate could include more than 50 underwriters. Their selection will reflect the geographic distribution targeted for your offering and the relative mix of institutional and retail investors anticipated or desired.

Each of the underwriters in the syndicate will agree to underwrite a certain number of your shares and will then begin to approach its customers to determine the degree of interest in your offering. A copy of the "red herring" is provided to each prospective investor, who may then "express interest" in your shares based on their expected price range. However, you are not permitted to make any sales, or accept any offers to buy, prior to the effective date of the offering.

Based on the success of each member of the underwriting syndicate in selling your shares, they may ultimately take delivery of more or fewer shares than they originally subscribed for. Allocation of the underwriting commission is first made to the managing underwriters as compensation for managing the offering, with the balance allocated to the underwriting syndicate in proportion to both the number of shares underwritten and the number of shares ultimately accepted for sale to investors.

Limited Selling Efforts
The SEC places various restrictions on what you may and may not do while your company is "in registration." These restrictions apply from the date you reach an understanding with your managing underwriters to handle your offering until 25 days after the securities are offered to the public (90 days for securities not listed on a national exchange or quoted on Nasdaq).

During the period prior to initial filing of the registration statement, the 1933 Act prohibits you from "offering" the security. The SEC has interpreted this phrase to include "the publication of information and statements, and publicity efforts, made in advance of a proposed financing that have the effect of conditioning the public mind or arousing public interest in the issuer or in its securities." However, this does not preclude the normal ongoing disclosure of factual information about the company. The SEC encourages companies to continue product advertising campaigns, periodic reporting to shareholders, and press announcements on factual business and financial developments, such as new contracts obtained and plant openings. However, you may not initiate new publicity or issue forecasts or projections of revenue, income, or earnings per share. To avoid the potentially serious consequences of violating the SEC rules, you should clear any press releases or public statements with your attorneys in advance.

Specific guidelines also have been established with respect to the period after filing of the registration statement. As already noted, the "red herring" prospectus may now be widely distributed to underwriters and the investing public. No other written sales literature is allowed. You may, however, publish a limited notice of the offering, including the amount of the offering, the name of the company, a description of the security, the offering price, and the names of the underwriters. Known as "tombstone ads" because of their stark appearance, these notices are typically published in newspapers shortly after the registration statement's announcement and are not considered sales literature. Exhibit 5–4 is an example "tombstone ad" that would appear in the financial press for a company's initial public offering.

Specified oral selling efforts are allowed once the initial registration statement is filed. Despite the comprehensive restrictions imposed by the SEC, most of the underwriters' sales efforts take place during this period. In addition to distributing your preliminary prospectus and soliciting "expressions of interest" from investors, your underwriters generally will take your executives on a traveling "road show," also referred to as a "dog-and-pony show." These meetings give prospective members of the underwriting syndicate, institutional investors, and industry analysts an opportunity to meet your company's management team and ask questions relating to your offering and your company. The tour may cover a number of cities, including those where the major members of the underwriting syndicate are located and where investor interest is expected to be greatest. And in today's global marketplace, depending on the size of the offering and the company, the tour may include presentations in select foreign countries.

In Regulation A offerings, the SEC will permit companies to "test the waters" for potential public interest in the company prior to the preparation or filing of the registration statement with the SEC. In these circumstances, companies are allowed to test the market through oral presentations as well as newspaper and other media advertisements. These communications have specific requirements and are not allowed in all states as a

EXHIBIT 5–4. Example of a "tombstone ad."

This announcement is neither an offer to sell nor a
solicitation to buy these securities.
The offer is made only by the Prospectus.

New Issue   **September 22, 1994**

2,500,000 Shares

Common Stock

Price $18.00 Per Share

Copies of the Prospectus may be obtained in any State in which this
announcement is circulated from only such of the undersigned or other
dealers or brokers as may lawfully offer these securities in such State.

XYZ SECURITIES CORP.

UNDERWRITER 1	UNDERWRITER 2	UNDERWRITER 3
MORE UNDERWRITERS	MORE UNDERWRITERS	MORE UNDERWRITERS
MORE UNDERWRITERS	MORE UNDERWRITERS	MORE UNDERWRITERS
MORE UNDERWRITERS	MORE UNDERWRITERS	MORE UNDERWRITERS
MORE UNDERWRITERS	MORE UNDERWRITERS	MORE UNDERWRITERS
MORE UNDERWRITERS	MORE UNDERWRITERS	MORE UNDERWRITERS
MORE UNDERWRITERS	MORE UNDERWRITERS	MORE UNDERWRITERS
MORE UNDERWRITERS	MORE UNDERWRITERS	MORE UNDERWRITERS
MORE UNDERWRITERS	MORE UNDERWRITERS	MORE UNDERWRITERS
MORE UNDERWRITERS	MORE UNDERWRITERS	MORE UNDERWRITERS
MORE UNDERWRITERS	MORE UNDERWRITERS	MORE UNDERWRITERS

result of more restrictive state laws. The "test the waters" provisions of Regulation A are more fully explained in Chapter 8.

Underwriting Agreement

The formal underwriting agreement is negotiated before filing and executed on the last day before the registration statement becomes effective. At this stage, the offering price and the number of shares (or amount of debt) to be offered are finalized. Changed market conditions and feedback from the underwriting syndicate may necessitate changes in the offering price or in the size of the offering. If market conditions have taken an unfavorable turn since the filing date, your underwriters may recommend a reduction in price or in the number of shares offered. In extreme cases, they may even advise a postponement of the offering. Conversely, you may find that you are able to increase the price or the size of the offering.

If all have agreed to proceed with the offering, deficiencies noted by the SEC have been cleared to their satisfaction, and the final pricing details have been agreed upon, the printer is instructed to print the final prospectus. The following morning the underwriting agreement is signed and the registration statement is declared effective.

The final settlement or "closing" is discussed later in this chapter.

STATE SECURITIES LAWS

In addition to filing a registration statement with the SEC and otherwise satisfying federal securities laws, your company also must comply with state securities laws in all states in which your securities will be offered. The impact of state securities laws can range from a simple notification requirement to a prohibition on selling your securities in the state, even if your registration statement has been reviewed by the SEC and is effective. Therefore, the various reporting, filing, and qualification requirements of the states in which you intend to offer your securities should be addressed early in the registration process.

State securities laws are known as "blue sky" laws, in reference to various fraudulent schemes common in the early 1900s which were characterized as selling building lots in the "blue sky." In response to these schemes, and to protect investors, many states enacted securities legislation. Unlike federal securities regulation, which is limited to ensuring the adequacy of disclosure, many state "blue sky" laws address the merit of offerings and disallow offerings not considered "fair, just, or equitable." The particular issues that some states consider in evaluating the merit of your offering include the price-earnings ratio; dilution to new shareholders; amount and terms of loans to existing shareholders, directors, and employees; and the voting rights of the offered shares.

The North American Securities Administrators' Association (NASAA) has developed guidelines for securities legislation that are designed to make the state registration process more uniform. However, because some states make their own evaluation of the merits of the offering, there will continue to be some lack of uniformity. NASAA "cheap stock" guidelines, as adopted by many of the states, require shares sold to promoters for less than the proposed offering price within the preceding three years to be held in escrow for several years. This escrow is subject to the success of the issuer's earnings and the performance of its stock in the public market.

Generally, once you have decided in which states your offering will be registered, the attorneys will prepare a Blue Sky Memorandum setting forth the various provisions and restrictions applicable to each of those states. This gives you time to plan how to deal with those provisions and to decide whether any other states should be excluded from the offering.

The mechanics of complying with state "blue sky" laws—filing notices, copies of the registration statement, or other information as required—generally will be handled by your underwriters' attorneys.

Additionally, before an offering becomes effective it must be cleared by the National Association of Securities Dealers (NASD). The purpose of the NASD review is to determine whether the underwriting agreement is fair and reasonable. The NASD examines both direct compensation (discount or commission) and indirect compensation (underwriter warrants or stock options, expense reimbursements) and also regulates certain other aspects of the underwriters' arrangements.

YOUR TIMETABLE AND EXPENSES

While it is difficult to generalize, few initial public offerings are completed in less than three months, and almost all are more expensive than any other source of financing. Differing circumstances affect the timing and costs of a public offering, but a brief review of the contributing factors may give you an idea of what to expect.

Timetable

Two to three months generally elapse from the date a company decides to make an initial public offering to the date the registration statement is initially filed with the SEC. The SEC staff then takes approximately 30 days to issue its first comment letter, but it may take longer to complete its initial review. A sample timetable for going public is included in Exhibit 5–2. The effective date of the registration statement can be as soon as two days after the SEC staff's comments are resolved.

The process begins with the first "all-hands" meeting, attended by all parties, including company executives, attorneys, auditors, underwriters, and underwriters' attorneys. At this meeting, preliminary discussions are held on the terms of the offering, the registration form to be used, and the financial statement requirements. The parties also establish a detailed timetable and assign responsibilities for preparing various portions of the registration statement.

Preparing the first draft of the registration statement can take 45 days or more. Once all assigned portions of the registration statement have been provided to your attorneys, they circulate a draft to all parties. At subsequent meetings the parties carefully review and discuss the draft and agree upon revisions.

The third "all-hands" meeting is attended by all parties. At this meeting, the printer's proof of the registration statement is reviewed and the signature pages completed.

Once the registration statement is filed with the SEC, the "road show" may begin. Company executives and managing underwriters meet with prospective investors and others to discuss the company and the offering.

As soon as the SEC comment letter is received, draft amendments are prepared to respond to SEC comments. If required, the prospectus information, including financial statements, is updated.

Finally, all parties meet again to review and approve the draft amendments and finalize the pricing. The final registration statement is then filed with the SEC, and if all SEC comments have been addressed to the satisfaction of the SEC staff, they will, at your request, declare the registration statement effective.

Expenses

The underwriters' discount or commission will be influenced by the size and structure of the offering. For example, debt offerings generally incur lower rates of commission than equity offerings. The commission also will depend on market conditions, competition for underwriting business, and the relative stability of your company and industry. A highly speculative offering may require more effort to sell and thus necessitate a higher rate of commission. Usually, the underwriters' commission for initial public offerings is in the range of 6 percent to 10 percent. Some underwriters also require you to pay some of their out-of-pocket expenses as well.

Legal fees generally represent the second largest expense. They include fees not only for preparation and review of the registration statement, but also for the various related tasks required in anticipation of a public offering, such as a review of contracts and other legal housecleaning chores.

Additionally, you are often required to pay the legal fees incurred by your underwriters' attorneys for their attorneys' review of compliance with state securities laws. Because of the complexities of these laws, the underwriters' attorneys often perform this work on your behalf. Fees can range from just a few thousand dollars to more than $100,000, depending on how many and in which states the offering will be made.

Printing costs usually exceed $50,000, and sometimes can reach over $150,000. Numerous revisions, a large press run, and the use of color photographs will contribute to higher printing costs.

Accounting fees can vary and depend significantly on whether audits have been performed in the past. The fees will also be affected by the relative strength of a company's system of internal controls, the ability of the internal reporting system to generate industry segment data and other required disclosure information for public companies, the timing of the offering and resulting need to include interim financial statements, as well as the extent of the procedures required in connection with the provision of a "comfort letter."

Other expenses include the SEC filing fee (1/29 of one percent of the maximum aggregate offering price), NASD filing fee ($500 plus .01 percent of the maximum aggregate offering price—$30,500 maximum fee), indemnity insurance premium (if required by underwriters, and if obtainable), state "blue sky" filing fees (the amount depends on number of states and size of offering), and registrar and transfer agent fees (generally at least $5,000).

The final element of cost is the heavy commitment of executive time required for an initial public offering. This time commitment begins with the selection of your underwriters and other professional advisors, continues throughout the registration statement preparation process, and may intensify during the "road shows" that precede the effective date of the offering. (The "road shows" themselves also can involve considerable expense.) Being a public company also will place demands on executives' time.

Awareness of the factors contributing to costs and time delays may enable you to take steps to control them. Following are some tips on saving time and money:

- **Underwriters' Compensation.** You should not select your managing underwriters based on their compensation. In negotiating with your underwriters, bear in mind the factors they consider in determining their fees. A well-prepared business plan will help "sell" your company to the underwriters and reduce the amount of effort needed to sell your shares. With smaller underwriters and for smaller offerings, you may be able to trade off commission percentage points for underwriter warrants. (Outstanding warrants increase the potential dilution of the shares being offered and thus may reduce the price you can obtain for your shares.) Also, the reimbursable amount of your underwriters' attorneys' fees for compliance with state securities laws depends largely on the number of states in which you register your offering.

- **Legal Fees.** You cannot avoid legal fees incurred directly for preparation of the registration statement, due diligence, and other related procedures. But fees for certain other legal services can be held to a minimum. For example, you can reduce the extent of required legal "house cleaning" by consulting regularly with legal counsel in the years preceding a public offering on such matters as employment contracts, employee stock option and award plans, and any other contracts that may present a problem when you decide to go public.

- **Accounting Fees.** The fees directly related to the registration process are unavoidable. These include review of financial information, attendance at "all-hands" meetings, reading prefiling drafts, assistance with responding to SEC comments, and the provision of comfort letters and related procedures. But often accounting fees are driven up by weak systems of internal control, inadequate internal reporting systems, and the absence of audit opinions on prior years' financial statements. Annual audits and reliable internal controls reduce both the time and expense of a public offering.

- **Printing Costs.** Excessive revisions are the biggest culprit in printing cost overruns. Keeping drafts in word processing format as long as possible will help reduce the number of printer's proofs required. Inevitably, some revisions will be made after the initial printer's proofs are obtained as items are challenged in the context of other disclosures, and in response to changing market conditions. But you can hold the number of revisions to a minimum by having all text, charts, diagrams, graphs, and even type style, format, and color approved in advance. Printer's proofs are expensive, especially in the context of the desired one-day turnaround and the overtime charges that may result. By appointing one individual to coordinate all comments and revisions, you can reduce the likelihood of overlooked comments and incomplete revisions and thus the number of printer's proofs.

- **SEC Review.** The time required for the initial SEC review of your registration statement is largely beyond your control. While the SEC's goal is to issue its first comment letter within 30 days of filing of the preliminary prospectus, this sometimes takes longer in times of heavy market activity. Delays, both in issuing the first comment letter and in resolving SEC concerns, also may be caused by your company's unwillingness to make certain disclosures, or by its use of inexperienced attorneys or auditors.

Overall, an initial public offering will be both time-consuming and expensive. But advance planning and preparation, careful selection of your professional advisors, and the cooperation of all parties can keep costs and delays to a minimum.

Amending the Registration Statement

The registration team should address *all* of the comments in the regulatory review response letters, either by amending the registration statement or by discussing with the SEC and state regulators the reasons why revisions are unnecessary and obtaining concurrence with that conclusion.

A draft of the amended registration statement is distributed to the registration team for review, any necessary changes are made (including updating the financial statements), and the amended registration statement is filed. After all the parties involved are satisfied with the technical and disclosure aspects of the registration statement, the pricing amendment is filed. The pricing amendment discloses the offering price, the underwriters' commission, and the net proceeds to the company.

Although technically there is a 20-day waiting period after the final registration statement is filed before it becomes effective, an "acceleration request" is usually filed concurrently with the pricing amendment. The request asks the SEC to waive the 20-day waiting period and declare the registration statement effective immediately.* The SEC usually approves acceleration requests.

After the registration statement becomes effective, the final prospectus is printed and distributed to everyone who received a copy of the preliminary prospectus and to others who expressed an interest in purchasing the stock.

The Closing

The registration process culminates with the company issuing the securities to the underwriters and receiving the proceeds (net of the underwriters' compensation) from the offering. The

---

*Acceleration is particularly critical in firm-commitment underwritings, because underwriters generally are unwilling to risk deterioration in the market after the offering price has been set.

closing for firm-commitment underwritings generally occurs five to seven business days after the registration statement becomes effective. The closing for best-efforts underwritings generally is 60 to 120 days after the effective date, provided the underwriters have sold at least the minimum number of shares specified in the registration statement.

6

AFTER THE OFFERING— BEING A PUBLIC COMPANY

Going public will subject your company, its shareholders, directors, and executives to a variety of new responsibilities. Some of these relate to the requirements of the securities laws, and others relate to the way you must now conduct your company's affairs. Some of the laws to which you are now subject are extremely technical and complex, and your attorneys and auditors will advise and assist you in complying with those provisions. The following is a brief overview of some of those requirements and responsibilities.

PERIODIC REPORTING

One of the first reports that must be filed after a registered public offering is a Form SR periodic report on the use of proceeds of the offering. A Form SR must be filed within 10 days after the end of the first three-month period following the effective date of the registration statement and then within 10 days of the end of each subsequent six-month period. A final report is due 10 days after the later of termination of the offering or application of the proceeds of the offering. Form SR is a short question-and-answer form on which you must report sales of securities, the use of the net proceeds, and whether the use of the proceeds is materially different from that described in the prospectus. If it is materially different, you must provide reasons for the change.

As a newly public company having filed a 1933 Act registration statement, you are also immediately subject to the 1934 Act periodic reporting requirements (pursuant to Section 15(d)) discussed next. Additionally, if your shares are to be traded on a national securities exchange or on Nasdaq, or if (at the end of the year) there are more than 500 shareholders of any class of your shares and the company reported more than $5 million in assets, you will need to register under the 1934 Act (pursuant to Sections 12(b) and 12(g), respectively). This registration is accomplished by filing a Form 8-A which incorporates most information by reference from the registration statement and periodic reports to the SEC. This registration will usually become effective after the national securities exchange has approved the listing application and notified the SEC.

Although you are required to file periodic reports for your first fiscal year, the duty to file such reports may be immediately suspended after the first fiscal year-end if, with respect to the class of securities registered, there are fewer than 300 shareholders. It will also be suspended if, after the first two fiscal years following the offering, there are fewer than 500 shareholders and the company reported less than $5 million in assets on the last day of each of the previous three years. The reporting suspension becomes effective immediately upon filing of Form 15 with the SEC. If your company's securities are listed on a national securities exchange or on Nasdaq, however, you are subject to the periodic reporting requirements regardless of the number of shareholders.

The importance of compliance with the periodic reporting requirements cannot be overemphasized. Periodic reports represent a primary form of communication with your shareholders and the financial community in general. Poorly prepared, incomplete, or late reports may adversely affect your investors and public relations. It may also lead to SEC sanctions, generate ill will toward your company by the SEC staff, and could even preclude future use of certain simplified registration forms. The required periodic reporting forms are discussed next.

Form 10-K

This is the primary report used annually to update much of the information contained in your original registration statement. The specific disclosure requirements are similar to those of the S-1 registration statement. As with the registration statement, the form itself is merely a guide, not a blank form to be filled in. Form 10-K is due within 90 days after the end of the fiscal year.

Much of the information required in Form 10-K is also required in various other SEC filings or in the annual report to shareholders prescribed by the SEC's proxy requirements (discussed below). Instead of including information that already has been included in previous SEC filings or an annual report to shareholders in the current Form 10-K, a company may incorporate that information into the Form 10-K by reference to the previously filed document or annual report to shareholders. For example, a company may include as an exhibit to the Form 10-K a copy of the annual report to shareholders containing the audited financial statements in lieu of reproducing the same financial statements in the 10-K.

Form 10-Q

The 10-Q quarterly report is a summarized report containing quarterly unaudited financial statements and management's discussion and analysis of financial condition and results of operations. Additionally, certain specified events (e.g., legal proceedings, changes in the terms of securities, certain defaults, and matters submitted to a shareholders' vote) need to be disclosed in the 10-Q. Form 10-Q must be filed within 45 days after the end of each of the first three fiscal quarters.

Form 8-K

This report is required to be filed after specified significant events, including change in control, significant acquisition or disposition of assets, bankruptcy or receivership, change in independent auditors, resignation of a director, or any other event considered of importance to shareholders. The form must be filed within 15 days of the reportable event, except in the case of a change in independent auditors or the resignation of a director (under certain circumstances), which must be reported within five business days. The form specifies certain minimum disclosures about each event.

Small Business Issuers

As explained in Chapter 8, small business issuers may elect to fulfill their quarterly and annual financial reporting requirements by filing Form 10-QSB and Form 10-KSB, respectively.

Periodic Reporting Requirements under the Securities Exchange Act of 1934

Upon completion of the IPO, a registrant becomes subject to the periodic reporting requirements under the 1934 Act. The required date and form for the registrant's first 1934 Act filing depends on whether the first report to be filed is a Form 10-Q or Form 10-K, and which 1934 Act rule governs the registrant's periodic reporting.

In situations where the first report to be filed by a new registrant is a Form 10-Q. Form 10-Q must be filed within 45 days of the effective date of the IPO registration statement, or on or before the date on which such report would have been required to have been filed had the registrant been required to file reports on Form 10-Q for its latest fiscal quarter, whichever is later. For example, an IPO for a calendar year registrant that is declared effective on July 15 ordinarily will include unaudited interim financial statements for the quarter ended March 31. In this circumstance, the new registrant's first Form 10-Q, covering the three- and six-month periods ended June 30, would be due August 29 (the 45th day following the effective date of the registration statement).

In situations where the first report to be filed by a new registrant is a Form 10-K, a determination of whether the registrant's reporting requirements are pursuant to Section 12 or Section 15 of the 1934 Act will impact the timing and type of report to be filed.

Registrants filing periodic reports under Section 12 of the 1934 Act must file their complete Form 10-K with the SEC within 90 days of their year end (Rule 13a-1 under the 1934 Act). Registrants filing periodic reports under Section 15 of the 1934 Act, whose IPO registration statement did not contain financial statements for the registrant's last full fiscal year (or life of the registrant if less than a full fiscal year) preceding the fiscal year in which the registration statement became effective shall, within 90 days after the effective date, file with the SEC a special report that includes only financial statements for such last full fiscal year or other period as the case may be, meeting the requirements of the form appropriate for annual reports of the registrant (Rule 15d-2 under the 1934 Act). This report shall contain only financial statements for the year in question (i.e., there is no requirement for any disclosures pursuant to Regulation S-K).

INVESTOR AND PUBLIC RELATIONS

As an officer or director of a new public company, you suddenly have acquired what may be described as a mixed blessing. As a result of the capital infusion into your company, you have acquired a group of shareholders, often numbering in the hundreds or thousands, each of whom has a valid and vital interest in your company's success. These shareholders, either directly or relying on securities analysts as well as the financial press, will critically evaluate your management's performance. Also, these shareholders will measure your company's progress against their own expectations and the performance of your competitors and your industry.

Your new responsibility to shareholders has far-reaching implications for the way you conduct your company's business.

Facing your company's owner no longer consists of a gaze in the mirror or a walk into the corner office. Your obligation to keep the owners informed of corporate developments must now be fulfilled through annual and quarterly reports, proxy statements, press releases, direct mailings, and shareholders' meetings.

A public company must promptly disclose any significant events or developments concerning the company, whether positive or negative. Particular care should be exercised that material information is disclosed publicly and not leaked intentionally or inadvertently.

A new measure of your company's performance has also been introduced—the company's share price. From the shareholders' perspective, this is the critical measure. New public companies often initially enjoy high share prices resulting, in part, from investor interest in initial public offerings and fueled by the press attention that often attends a company's going public.

Unless that market interest in your company is sustained after the public offering, the initial euphoria will disappear and the value of your company's shares will decline. Maintaining your company's positive image with the financial community, and market interest in your shares, requires a conscious effort by management.

Investor Relations

To maintain market interest in your securities, you should direct your efforts not only at existing investors in your company—the shareholders—but also at potential investors. Various media can be used effectively to reach this financial community.

Securities analysts play a vital role in the financial community. They are often part of the research departments of brokerage houses and investment banking arms, and so their assessments of your company will influence the investment advice provided to their investor clients. Securities analysts not only will analyze your annual reports and other published information, but will also conduct interviews with your company's management to gain insight into your operations, plans, and prospects. Your company's management should welcome such interviews, and even initiate them where possible.

Many cities have local societies or groups of securities analysts who meet regularly to hear presentations by public companies' management. These forums give management an opportunity to promote the company, disseminate information on its plans, and respond to analysts' questions. Opportunities to appear before these groups should be welcomed.

Many companies prepare a corporate brochure and update it regularly in connection with security analyst presentations and for general corporate publicity. These brochures may include a description of the company and its products or services, a brief history of the company, information on its management team, selected financial data, and any other information considered relevant.

Public Relations

Maintaining a strong, positive corporate image will serve your company well. In addition to reinforcing your image with shareholders and potential investors, it will help attract and retain employees, influence customer and consumer purchase decisions, and create goodwill that may indirectly benefit your company in a variety of ways.

Many companies retain public relations consultants to assist them. A good public relations program can be integrated with product advertising, but should also be directed at developing a corporate image beyond the company's specific products or services.

Short-Term Profits and Long-Term Growth

One of the ever-present issues facing public companies is the pressure to maintain short-term earnings growth. There is often a temptation to maintain share prices by sacrificing long-term profitability and growth for short-term earnings. The financial markets generally react adversely to reduced earnings reports,

whether or not they result from sound long-term strategic decisions. This unfortunate dilemma does not imply that investors
are shortsighted. Rather, it reflects the realities of the financial
markets and emphasizes the need for a strong investor relations
program.

John Maynard Keynes, the noted economist, likened professional investment decisions to "those newspaper competitions
in which the competitors have to pick out the six prettiest faces
from a hundred photographs, the prize being awarded to the
competitor whose choice most nearly corresponds to the average preferences of the competitors as a whole; so that each competitor has to pick, not those faces which he himself finds
prettiest, but those which he thinks likeliest to catch the fancy
of the other competitors, all of whom are looking at the problem from the same point of view. It is not a case of choosing
those which, to the best of one's judgment, are really the prettiest, nor even those which average opinion genuinely thinks the
prettiest." He noted that "we have reached the third degree
where we devote our intelligence to anticipating what average
opinion expects the average opinion to be."

There is no easy solution to this dilemma. But you should
strive to adopt a sound business strategy balanced between
short- and long-term needs, and communicate that strategy to
shareholders and the financial community.

COMPLIANCE WITH THE LAW

As a public company, you will now be subject to a variety of laws
and regulations—in addition to the periodic reporting requirements noted above—which did not apply when you were a private company.

Proxy Solicitation

Because the shareholders of most public companies are widely
dispersed and because few attend shareholders' meetings,

management of a company usually solicits from shareholders the authority to vote their stock (solicit their proxies) at the annual shareholders' meeting. Proxies typically account for the majority of votes cast at shareholders' meetings.

The SEC requires that, before proxies may be solicited, a proxy statement must first be provided to shareholders. The content of the proxy statement is specified in the SEC regulations, and varies according to the matters to be voted on. If directors are to be elected, an annual report including financial statements must also be provided. Even if management does not solicit proxies, an information statement similar in content to a proxy statement must be furnished to shareholders. However, companies listed on the New York or American stock exchanges are required by those exchanges to solicit proxies. Also, the NASD requires national market system issuers with securities quoted on Nasdaq to solicit proxies for all shareholder meetings.

The proxy rules apply only to companies that are subject to the 1934 Act because they are listed on a national exchange, or because they have more than 500 shareholders and $5 million in assets (i.e., reporting under Section 12). They do not apply to unlisted companies that do not meet the size test and are subject to the 1934 Act only by virtue of a 1933 Act registered public offering (i.e., reporting under Section 15(d)).

Tender Offers and Reports by Shareholders with 5 Percent Ownership

The SEC regulates both the mechanics for making tender offers and the procedures for management's resisting tender offers. Additionally, shareholders or groups of shareholders acting together who acquire 5 percent or more of your company's shares, or who make a tender offer that would result in 5 percent or more ownership, are subject to specified disclosure requirements. Reports must be filed with the SEC and provided to your company and any stock exchanges on which the shares are listed. The reports must provide specified information, generally including the identity and background of the purchaser(s), the source and amount of funds used in the purchase, the purpose of the transaction, and the number of shares owned. As with the proxy solicitation rules, the tender offer rules do not apply to companies subject to the 1934 Act only by virtue of a 1933 Act registered public offering.

Insider Trading and "Short-Swing Profits"

All directors and officers, as well as shareholders with 10 percent or more of your company's shares, are required to report their holdings to the SEC on specified forms and within certain time limits. Any subsequent changes in those holdings must likewise be reported.

To prevent the unfair use of insider information, these insiders are also subject to the "short-swing profits" provisions of the 1934 Act. The provisions apply to any profits realized by insiders on the purchase and sale, or sale and purchase, of any of your company's securities within a six-month period, whether or not those transactions were based on insider information. These insiders are required to turn over to the company an amount equal to the difference between the highest sale price and the lowest purchase price within the six-month period, without any offset for losses. And if the company does not sue the insider to recover those profits, any shareholder may do so on behalf of the company.

The 1934 Act also prohibits insiders from selling shares that they do not own (i.e., "short" sales) and from selling shares that they own but do not deliver within 20 days after the sale (i.e., "short sales against the box").

It is also unlawful for anyone to trade in a company's securities on the basis of insider information. This applies equally to those directly privy to the insider information (e.g., directors, officers, employees) and to anyone whom they "tip off" regarding such information before it is made public. Both the insider (whether or not he or she benefits personally) and the "tippee" may be subject to liability for damages to everyone who traded in the security during the period of such illegal insider trading.

Therefore, as a public company you should take appropriate measures to provide reasonable assurance that controls are in place to protect the confidentiality of such sensitive information, and that anyone who must become privy to such information is made aware of the proscription on trading on or conveying such information. It may also be advisable to coordinate all press statements and communications with analysts, reporters, and other public communications through a single individual.

Sale of Restricted and Control Stock—Rule 144

As noted earlier, controlling shareholders are not free to sell their shares in the public markets at will, but must sell them either through a registered secondary offering or in reliance on a specified exemption. Similarly, shares acquired in most private placements (e.g., Regulation D offerings—discussed in Chapter 8) are considered "restricted stock" and are subject to resale restrictions intended to ensure that the private placement was not simply one step in a broader public distribution.

To clarify the restrictions on sales of restricted and control stock, the SEC adopted Rule 144 in 1972. Rule 144 provides a "safe harbor" for such sales. Essentially, it allows controlling shareholders, and holders of restricted stock who have held the stock for two years after it was fully paid, to sell up to the greater of the following in any three-month period:

- One percent of the securities of that class outstanding, or
- The average weekly trading volume, if the security is listed on a national exchange or quoted on Nasdaq.

Restricted stock not held by controlling shareholders becomes free of most resale restrictions after a three-year holding period, again measured from the date the stock was fully paid. Note, however, that the SEC has interpreted payment in full to exclude, for example, certain notes accepted in payment under stock option or stock purchase plans.

Other provisions relate to combining sales of certain affiliated persons for purposes of the rule, limitations on brokerage commissions, and SEC notification requirements for sales in excess of 500 shares or $10,000 in a three-month period. Because the provisions of Rule 144 are complex, you should consult your attorneys with respect to any proposed sales under the rule.

EXCHANGE LISTING VS. NASDAQ LISTING

In the past, almost all companies going public hoped eventually to be listed on the New York or American stock exchanges. That is no longer the case.

Today, in increasing numbers, companies that would qualify for listing on a floor-based market choose to have their securities listed on the Nasdaq National Market, a screen-based market. New public companies must now consider the relative differences of exchange listing versus a Nasdaq listing:

- Marketability and collateral value are generally perceived to be enhanced by a stock exchange listing because market values can be readily determined and transactions can be consummated more quickly. However, the Nasdaq National Market offers the same real-time trade reporting and automated transaction confirmation, and it enables buyers and sellers to be matched just as quickly.

- A certain prestige is undoubtedly attached to companies listed on a national securities exchange. The extent to which that perception influences decisions by investors, analysts, creditors, and others is open to question. On the other hand, Nasdaq has come to be associated with growth companies and those that are technologically advanced.

- Published security prices in major newspapers were previously limited generally to listed companies. Major newspapers now also print similar information for many Nasdaq National Market securities.

- Some institutional investors are limited to investing only in national exchange securities while others may be more attracted to these securities. To the extent that stock exchange listing increases the marketability of large blocks of shares, institutional investors may be more inclined to invest in these securities.

Moreover, companies must meet qualification requirements for listing on a national exchange or the Nasdaq National Market. The prestigious New York Stock Exchange requires, for example, pretax earnings of $2.5 million in the latest fiscal year and market value of listed securities of at least $18 million. It also has minimum requirements with respect to the number of shares outstanding, trading volume, and the number of shareholders. Companies listed on the exchange are also subject to the provisions of their listing agreement, which deals with such matters as timely disclosure and proxy solicitation.

The listing requirements and obligations imposed by the American Stock Exchange and the regional exchanges are generally less extensive than they are for the New York Stock Exchange or the Nasdaq National Market.

If you decide to have your company's securities listed on Nasdaq, you should consider seeking a Nasdaq National Market listing. A Nasdaq National Market listing increases the visibility of your securities and may broaden their attractiveness to institutional investors. To qualify, your company must satisfy various shareholder reporting, independent director, and audit committee requirements, and it must meet certain quantitative criteria, including minimums on the number of publicly held shares and market value.

Exhibit 6–1 contains the listing requirements for the New York Stock Exchange, American Stock Exchange, and Nasdaq National Market and Small Cap over-the-counter markets. An expanded discussion of choosing between exchange listing versus over-the-counter trading is included in Appendix A.

EXHIBIT 6–1. Major Listing Requirements (as of October 1994).

	Exchange-Based		Over-the-Counter	
	NYSE[a]	Amex	Nasdaq National Market	Nasdaq Small Cap
Distribution:				
Number of shareholders	2,200	800[b]	400[g]	300
Number of publicly held shares (thousands)	1,100	500[b]	500[g]	100[g]
Market value of public float (millions)	$ 18[g]	$ 3[g]	$ 3[g]	$ 1
Minimum bid price per share		$ 3	$ 5[g]	$ 3[g]
Market makers			2	2
Average monthly trading requirements (thousands)	100			
Size and Earnings:				
Net worth (millions)[c]	$ 18	$ 4	$ 4	$ 2[f]
Total assets (millions)				$ 4[f]
Pretax income (millions):[h]				
Latest year	$ 2.5	$ .75[d]	$ .75[d]	
Minimum each of the preceding 2 years	$ 2			
Directors:				
Minimum number of outside independent directors	2	2	2	
Audit committee required	Yes	Yes	Yes	No
Fees:[e]				
Original listing	$102,100	$37,500	$42,500	$10,000
Annual fee	$ 16,170	$11,000	$ 9,750	$ 4,000

[a] Companies may register on the NYSE if the company has 2,000 shareholders that own 100 or more shares rather than satisfying the number of shareholders, number of publicly held shares and the avararge monthly trading requirements.

[b] Alternatively, listing 400 stockholders and 1,000,000 public shares or 400 stockholders, 500,000 public shares and 2,000 shares of average daily volume.

[c] Net worth is defined as net tangible assets, except for the Amex, where it is stockholders' equity and Nasdaq Small Cap where it is capital and surplus.

[d] Alternatively, $750,000 for 2 of most recent 3 years.

[e] May vary based on the number of shares outstanding—for purposes of this table, it was assumed that 10 million shares were outstanding.

[f] Amounts are half for continuing inclusion. Amounts presented above are for initial inclusion.

[g] Additional rules or alternatives may apply—see the applicable guide, manual or by laws for details.

[h] Alternatively, companies may satisfy the pretax income requirement if their pretax income aggregated $6,500,000 for the last three years (and all years were profitable) with at least $4,500,000 earned during the most recent year.

7

ALTERNATIVE SOURCES OF FINANCING

Going public is not always the right answer. A wide variety of alternative sources of financing may be available for your company. Which source is best for you will depend on many different factors, including the amount required, when it is required, how long you expect to need it and when you can repay it, whether you can afford to service it, the stage in your company's development, and your goals and objectives.

This chapter presents just a few of the alternatives available, and briefly examines the advantages and disadvantages of each. Included are examples of two types of financing: equity (private placements, strategic partnerships, ESOPs) and debt (commercial lenders, leasing, the Small Business Administration, and Small Business Investment Companies). We will also discuss two sources of "bridge financing" that can be used to meet your needs until the time is right for an initial public offering. Finally, we will review the option of selling or merging your company— an alternative to consider if your reason for going public is to liquidate your investment.

Some of the alternatives discussed may not be available to you, while others may not suit your corporate and personal objectives. But perhaps one of these alternatives will suit your needs better than a public offering, or will satisfy those needs temporarily until you go public. In any event, they should be considered and weighed carefully as you decide whether to go public.

PRIVATE PLACEMENTS
(EXEMPT OFFERINGS OF SECURITIES)

Many entrepreneurs at the head of small and growing companies dream of taking their companies public not only as a means of raising capital for growth, but for two other enticing advantages: The prestige of being a public company and the considerable financial gain earlier investors can often realize. But what if this is not the time?

Going public will be feasible eventually, but how can your company obtain needed financing now? Selling stock directly to private investors can be faster and less expensive than a public stock offering. Through an exempt offering, commonly called a private placement, you can offer stock to private investors without most of the detailed and time-consuming SEC registration requirements.

A private placement is "exempt" from filing a registration statement with the SEC. This is a significant advantage because it reduces paperwork, saves time, and costs far less than an IPO. A private placement is so called because you can offer the stock or debt to a few private investors instead of the public at large.

In addition, raising capital in the private markets can enable you to maintain the control and most of the confidentiality you enjoy as the owner/manager of a private company.

Saving time and money for small companies in need of growth capital was exactly what Congress had in mind when it spelled out these exemptions in the 1933 Act. The aim was to simplify compliance with securities laws and make it easier for companies to raise capital. The Small Business Investment Incentive Act of 1980 expanded exempt-offering opportunities, and the resulting changes in SEC regulations have made private placements an increasingly popular method of raising capital. The SEC's 1992 Small Business Initiatives further simplified and expanded the exempt-offering process.

While "exemption" is the key word, you have far from a completely free hand. For one thing, while your private placement may be exempt from federal registration, it may not be exempt from registration under state laws. Some states require registration, some do not. Also, private placements are not exempt from antifraud provisions of the securities laws. This means that you must give potential investors the necessary information about your company to make a well-informed decision. You must exercise meticulous care not to omit or misstate the facts or give them a rosier hue than they deserve.

When to Consider a Private Placement

There are other considerations in a private placement, as your attorney or independent accountant will tell you. Broadly defined, the private placement market includes a wide variety of larger corporate finance transactions, including senior and subordinated debt, asset-backed securities, and equity issues. This sophisticated, highly developed market is dominated by institutional investors (including insurance companies, pension funds, and money management funds), larger corporate issuers, and investment bankers or other corporate finance intermediaries. In recent years, debt financing in the institutional market totaled over $50 billion in the United States. Equity financing, though smaller in dollar volume, is also substantial. If your company is contemplating a debt financing of $10 million to $15 million or an equity financing of $5 million to $10 million, your financial advisor can help you determine whether the institutional market is a viable alternative.

As privately negotiated transactions, private placements can be designed to meet the specific needs of your company. Debt securities can have amortization schedules tailored to match anticipated cash flow. By attaching warrants or other equity "kickers," you can improve returns on debt securities for investors while not causing any immediate dilution or control implications for current ownership. Equity financing has the advantage of requiring no current servicing, thus conserving the company's cash flow for investment in the business. Creative securities can be structured to minimize the transfer of control to outside investors.

While private placements can involve debt, equity, or both, this chapter focuses on the registration exemptions for small issuers emphasizing equity transactions. We discuss why you might undertake a private placement, who the potential investors might be, and the types of exempt offerings that you should understand before you decide to proceed.

Private Placement Capital Sources

Compared with a public offering, your private placement will probably involve only a few investors. Individuals who already know and respect your company are the most likely and accessible investors. Consider targeting suppliers, dealers, franchisees, wholesalers, customers, and current shareholders. Many investment banking arms arrange private placements for emerging businesses and can connect you with individual investors, institutions, or foreign investors. If you know enough people and feel comfortable personally laying your proposition before them, fine. More likely, you will place the job of finding investors in the hands of a broker or financial advisor who makes a business of keeping track of investors who are willing to take risks with small companies.

Your other business advisors may also be helpful, especially in introducing you to potential investors. For example, they may introduce you to individuals who are indirectly affected by your industry but do not compete in it, thereby stimulating interest in your product or service, and therefore in your company.

SEC and state regulations limit the number and qualifications of the investors to whom you can offer your stock and, in some cases, the total amount you can raise in any one offering. There are also restrictions on the subsequent resale of these shares.

The resale restrictions, as well as the absence of a public market, often mean that the share price in a private placement will be lower than it is in a public offering. However, depending on your personal and corporate goals, as well as capital requirements, a private placement can be a viable financing alternative to an initial public offering. Private placements are described in more detail in Appendix D.

There are at least two different groups of investors that might have a special interest in your situation:

1. Suppose you manufacture a product and sell it to dealers, franchisers, or wholesalers. These are the people who know and respect your company. Moreover, they depend on you to supply the product they sell. They might consider it to be in their own self-interest to buy your stock if they believe it will help assure continuation of product supply.

    One problem with this type of arrangement is when one dealer invests and another does not; can you treat both fairly in the future? Another problem is that a customer who invests might ask for exclusive rights to market your product in a particular geographical area, and you might find it hard to refuse.

2. Private placements also often attract venture capitalists who hope to benefit when the company goes public or when the company is sold. To help assure that happy development, these investors get intimately involved at the board of directors level, where their skill and experience can help the company reach its potential.

    These professional investors are often focused on a particular industry, a specific geographic area, or companies at a defined development stage. Examples are prominent in fields such as high technology or biotechnology. Many professional investors or funds invest in companies that have developed products but need to build manufacturing capacity. If your situation matches the investors' criteria, and your management team is strong enough to stand up to the intensive scrutiny that is typical of professional investors, this may be a good source of private capital for your company.

Whatever the source of private capital, it is critical for the future growth and development of the company that the current owner and the new investors share a common outlook on the eventual exit strategy for the investors. Shared expectations with respect to the timing and structure of a public offering, a recapitalization financing, or the sale of the company to a larger corporation are as important to both the entrepreneur and the investors as the terms and conditions of the private placement.

STRATEGIC PARTNERSHIPS

Regardless of the label—strategic partnership, strategic alliance, or corporate venture—a collaboration with a larger, financially stronger company can provide you with the resources to meet your goals. A strategic partnership can contribute more than money to your company's success. Depending on your circumstances, your partner also might provide, for example, manufacturing or technological capabilities, or marketing agreements giving you access to new or expanded distribution channels, particularly in international markets.

Although almost any structure is possible, a typical strategic partnership involves the sale of a minority interest in your business to a larger company. In addition to equity, your partner may also expect to benefit from your entrepreneurial talent and ability to innovate. The partner might gain access to your technology, add your product to its product line, or profit from a business opportunity you have identified. Because of these benefits, a strategic partner is likely to require a smaller share of your equity than an investor seeking only a financial return on investment.

Several issues are critical to the success of your strategic partnership. Surveys of corporate partners indicate that the three most common causes of failed alliances are incompatible partners, unrealistic expectations, and ill-defined objectives.

In evaluating compatibility, partners should consider management and corporate styles and individual personalities. For example, how can an entrepreneurial partner—accustomed to quick actions—best work with a large firm with a slower, multilayered, decision-making process? Where will control be focused, and how will conflicts be resolved?

Both parties should assess their objectives and expectations and communicate them in a formal, written agreement. Issues such as timing, measurement criteria for determining the success of the project or relationship, and alternatives for ending the relationship should be defined up front and quantified to the extent possible.

Disappointment also occurs when the smaller partner learns that the larger partner might not be the source of the *unlimited* funding initially expected. Again, quantifiable milestones are important to provide realistic expectations. The ultimate success of a partnership requires compatible economic and strategic goals.

Your search for a strategic partner should start with the companies with whom you are already doing business. Major customers, suppliers, distributors, entrepreneurs, and other industry contacts are likely candidates. Don't forget referrals from investors, investment bankers, auditors, and lawyers who work with companies in your industry.

EMPLOYEE STOCK OWNERSHIP PLANS

If, in addition to raising capital, your goals include liquidity, estate planning, and employee motivation, you may want to consider an employee stock ownership plan (ESOP). An ESOP is a tax-favored type of employee benefit plan (a separate legal entity) to which your company makes annual contributions similar to other benefit plans. In an externally leveraged ESOP, the ESOP obtains a commercial loan, using the company contributions to service the debt. With the loan proceeds, the ESOP purchases your company's stock and maintains it for the employees' retirement benefits.

The intent of Congress in allowing ESOPs was to provide an incentive for companies to structure their financing so employees can gain a share of ownership. Thus, an ESOP is an effective way to provide equity capital without going public.

Within limits, the entire contribution to the ESOP is tax deductible; in effect, your company is paying both the interest and principal on this debt with pretax dollars. Dividends paid on shares owned by the ESOP also may be deductible.

In certain situations, banks, insurance companies, and other commercial lenders can exclude 50 percent of their interest income from their taxable income on loans to a qualified ESOP if the ESOP will own 50 percent of the company. As a result, lenders may be willing to make an ESOP-related loan at more favorable interest rates.

Because the ESOP is an employee benefit, the most cost-effective approach is to substitute it for another benefit plan, or reduce other forms of compensation to your employees. Most ESOPs do not acquire more than a minority interest in the outstanding stock of their companies, so you can still maintain control over your company.

An ESOP is not just a financing device but will have an ongoing effect on your company's operations and employees. Thus, if your only reason for establishing an ESOP is to raise capital, you may be better off obtaining a conventional loan.

Current accounting literature requires employers to measure compensation expense based on the fair value of the shares at the date they are released to the employees. Additionally, dividends paid on unallocated shares held by an ESOP must be charged to expense. Shares not yet committed to be released are not considered outstanding in earnings per share calculations.

COMMERCIAL LENDERS

You may think of your existing lenders only in terms of your current working capital needs. But they also could be the quickest source of additional expansion funds. Despite media focus on the "credit crunch" resulting from stricter regulatory credit requirements, new vehicles and more creative and exciting techniques have allowed "traditional" banks (as distinguished from bank-owned small business investment companies discussed later in this chapter) and other commercial lenders to remain a frequent source of financing for smaller businesses.

As your company grows, the number of debt alternatives available to you should also increase. Banks that turned you down during the company's early stages now may be interested because you can offer tangible assets for collateral and demonstrate adequate cash flow for servicing principal and interest payments. You should also determine whether you can gain access to additional funds (and/or more favorable terms) by restructuring your current banking arrangement.

Commercial finance companies may also seek smaller company customers. Finance companies (as well as many banks) provide asset-based financing, secured by your company's accounts receivable, inventory, equipment, or real estate. Because of the higher risk and costs associated with monitoring your collateral, however, the interest rate is higher for this type of loan than it is for a traditional bank loan.

The insurance industry provides another financing source for growing companies. If your company is profitable and meets certain financial milestones, an insurance company can provide capital to retire short-term debt; expand real estate, plant, and equipment; or make acquisitions. Typical loans from an insurance company are for a 10- to 20-year term, and therefore represent "semipermanent" capital. Additionally, these loans are generally unsecured, which frees your assets for additional borrowings.

LEASING

Leasing, a popular way of financing, offers a host of advantages and can be structured in various ways. Many companies lease their equipment, rather than purchase it, to avoid the initial cash outlay or assumption of debt. Depending on the terms of the lease, they may avoid the repair and maintenance costs of ownership, and may have more flexibility to upgrade or update the equipment as their needs change or technological improvements occur in available equipment. There is, of course, a price associated with these benefits. The lease payments reflect interest

costs as well as any costs of maintenance, credit risk, obsoles-
cence risk, and a profit factor. But these costs, spread over the
lease term, may be worth the immediate cash savings.

Another form of lease financing is, in essence, similar to secured borrowing. Leasing companies will either purchase new
equipment on your behalf and lease it to you (a direct financing lease) or purchase your existing equipment and lease it back
to you (a sale-leaseback). Typically, you avoid the cash outflow
of a purchase (or enjoy the cash inflow of a sale-leaseback), but
retain the other obligations of ownership—including repair,
maintenance, and insurance costs. You also remain at risk with
respect to the residual value, because ownership of the leased
equipment reverts to you at the end of the lease term.

The tax consequences of leasing transactions are complex, so
be sure to obtain the assistance of your tax advisors before entering into such transactions.

SMALL BUSINESS ADMINISTRATION

The Small Business Administration (SBA) is an agency of the federal government established by Congress to encourage and assist
small businesses. In addition to its management counseling services, the SBA assists many small businesses by guaranteeing a
qualifying loan or, in some cases, even granting a loan directly.

As with most government programs, various qualifications
must be met and restrictions are imposed. For example, the SBA
may extend loans or loan guarantees only to companies unable
to obtain financing from private sources. Thus, you must be
turned down by at least one bank (or more depending on the size
of your city) before approaching the SBA. There is also a ceiling
on the amount the SBA may lend to any one company, and on the
amount it may guarantee, which is generally limited to the lesser
of 90 percent of the loan or the dollar amount ceiling.

Despite these limitations, an SBA loan or loan guarantee can
be an attractive source of financing at a competitive rate for
those companies that qualify.

SMALL BUSINESS INVESTMENT COMPANIES

Licensed and partially funded by the SBA, Small Business Investment Companies (SBICs) take various forms. Some are independent private companies, while others are associated with venture capitalists or institutions such as banks and insurance companies. Because they are funded largely through loans from the SBA, the types of investments they can make are limited both legally and practically. They lend to or invest in small businesses qualifying for SBA assistance, and generally emphasize medium-term or long-term loans reflecting their own SBA debt structure.

Limits are placed on the interest rate they may charge on loans, which in turn limits the income earned for their shareholders. To boost their profits, and because they are allowed favorable tax treatment on capital gains, SBICs also usually take equity positions in the companies they lend to. Although they generally do not provide equity financing exclusively, they often structure a package to include preferred stock, options on shares, or debentures convertible into common shares. Because the SBA prohibits them from taking a controlling interest in any client company, you do not have to worry about losing control of your company to the SBIC investor.

Companies qualifying for SBIC loans can realize many advantages. Interest rates are usually reasonable, the loan term must exceed five years, and SBICs are flexible in developing a mutually acceptable financing package. And because they are generally experienced in dealing with small businesses, the investors can often provide you with significant ongoing management advice. Some SBICs charge a fee for advice, others provide it for free, and still others insist on providing it through board representation.

Although they are partially funded by a government agency, SBICs are still private businesses out to earn a profit. You must approach them in the same way as you would any other investor—well prepared, and with a detailed business plan. Literally hundreds of SBICs are operating in the United States today. Some specialize in specific industries, while others prefer certain types of financing packages. Therefore, before approaching any particular SBIC, you should find out what industry it specializes in and whether its preferred financing approach is consistent with your needs.

The biggest drawback in dealing with many SBICs is the limitation on the amount of financing they can provide. Most SBIC loans are less than $500,000, although larger loans can also be negotiated, often through syndication among several SBICs. However, each individual SBIC may not lend more than 20 percent of its capital to any one company. Thus, the maximum amount that can be financed is limited by the size of each SBIC in the syndicate. For larger amounts, you may have better success with one of the SBICs affiliated with a major bank.

BRIDGE CAPITAL FOR A FUTURE PUBLIC OFFERING

Regardless of the alternatives, you may decide that the rewards of going public exceed the risks, or a public offering may be necessary because of the magnitude of your capital requirements. However, even if you decide that going public is the best way to achieve your goals, the "window" for a public offering may be closed when you need it most. For example, market conditions may be unacceptable, or your company may be a year or two away from achieving the size, earnings, and growth profile necessary for an advantageous offering.

If you or the market are not quite ready for a public offering, you probably will need capital to sustain your growth in the meantime. "Bridge" capital—financing provided to a company expecting to go public within six months to two years—may be the answer. This type of financing is often structured to be repaid from the proceeds of the anticipated public offering.

Almost any financing alternative—private placements, for example—can be used as bridge financing. Two sources most often associated with bridge financing are discussed next—venture capitalists and mezzanine financing.

Venture Capitalists

Because they focus on future potential, venture capital firms often invest in companies that do not qualify for other forms of financing. As a result, venture capital is most appropriate for a fast-growth business with the potential to generate the exceptional returns these investors expect.

However, bear in mind the basic nature of a venture capital relationship. That is, at some point in the future, the venture capitalist supplying the funds will want to "harvest," or cash in on its investment.

Venture capital can take the form of common stock, preferred stock convertible into common stock, or debentures convertible into common stock. Whatever the form of the financial package, it is structured to allow the venture capitalists to liquidate their investment and realize their profits when the investment matures—which they usually expect within three to seven years. Some agreements call for a public offering after a specified number of years or at the venture capitalist's option. Others provide for a management buyout option, and still others result in the company being merged into or purchased by another company.

How active or passive a role the venture capitalist plays will vary. Because their investment in the company is predicated on confidence in existing management and the company's potential, they typically do not take over the company's management. However, when serving as the lead investor, they closely monitor the company's performance and frequently require board representation—which is often a blessing because venture capitalists generally have the business experience to make a meaningful contribution to the company. But should management fail to perform up to the promised and expected standards, venture capitalists generally do not hesitate to move in to protect their investment.

Approaching a venture capitalist may require some additional preparation beyond that required for other sources of financing. Recognizing their focus on your particular product or service, and their prospective equity stake in its success, you will want to provide detailed plans and projections. Your plan should explicitly specify the amounts and timing of financing requirements, the applications of all such funds, year-by-year (and month-by-month for the first one or two years) sales and profit projections, the projected time frame for completion or maturity of the venture, and how the venture capitalist will liquidate the investment and realize a profit. In preparing for the negotiations, you should also carefully consider how much of the company's equity you and the current shareholders are willing to give up, both now and in the future.

Many venture capital firms concentrate on specific industries or stages of investment, such as bridge financing. The valuable contacts, market expertise, and business strategy they can offer as a result of this specialization can be as important to you as the money they provide, so it is important to find potential investors whose skills, experience, goals, and reputations complement yours.

Mezzanine Financing

If your company is beyond the early growth stage but lacks the resources from earnings to fund sales growth or capital projects, mezzanine financing may solve your dilemma.

Although the term can be used to refer to any private placement of medium-risk capital, mezzanine financing often describes a subordinated debt instrument used by companies with sales of $5 million to $100 million.

In addition to a fixed interest rate, the debt comes with warrants to purchase equity in your company —typically 5 percent to 15 percent. Therefore, a lender may be willing to provide this type of financing to a company considered too high risk for conventional debt.

Although the fixed interest rate may be relatively low, the interest combined with the equity provision is designed to give the investor a total return of 20 percent to 30 percent—higher than you would pay for collateralized or other senior debt, but lower than the rate-of-return requirements of a typical venture capital investor.

Also, the mezzanine investor, like the venture capital investor, will want to cash in the investment at some point. Usually, this will be accomplished through a buy-back provision. You must determine whether you will be able to go public or how you will otherwise fund the buy-back.

Several mezzanine capital funds, structured similarly to venture capital funds, specialize in this stage of capital. A variety of other financial institutions also provide mezzanine financing, including insurance companies, finance companies, and banks.

SALE OR MERGER

If your reason for considering a public offering is to liquidate your investment, keep in mind that going public does not provide you with an immediate exit from your company. There are restrictions on the number of shares controlling shareholders can sell after a public offering. Selling or merging your company are more direct means of achieving liquidation.

Selling can provide quicker liquidity if you want to cash out or if you want to remain in the business but lower your risk by reducing your ownership stake. Additionally, a sale or merger can bring the resources your company needs to take advantage of other business opportunities that might present themselves. For example, larger corporations often search for acquisition opportunities for the same reasons they look for strategic partnerships, and this might provide new opportunities for you or your company.

In addition to other corporations, another potential buyer for your company might be your current management group. Leveraged buyouts by management—acquisitions of existing companies using a high proportion of institutional debt—frequently have been turned to as a way for management to participate in the purchase of a company. This transaction is most appropriate if your company has significant assets that can serve as collateral for debt used in its acquisition.

At first glance, selling your company might seem entirely different from completing a public offering; however, both require advance planning, marketing, and the establishment of a team of professionals. As with a public offering, a sale or merger must be timed to coincide with good corporate performance.

Pricing is an obvious consideration in a sale. But just as important are the method and timing of payment, as well as the extent of your future involvement with the company. Are you receiving cash up front, or will the final purchase price be based on future earnings? Will you be tied to the company with employment or noncompetition agreements?

The only way to decide whether to sell your business is by reflecting on your personal goals. Many entrepreneurs rarely consider how they will harvest their investment and years of hard work and therefore do not plan for it. To maximize your own returns, do not exclude the possibility of a future sale or merger as you plan your strategies today.

CONCLUSION

In deciding which financing alternatives are best for you at any particular growth stage, draw upon the experience of others who have already been through what you are encountering now. This includes other entrepreneurs, investment bankers, auditors, and other professionals.

Your financing strategy should be driven by your corporate and personal goals, your business strategy, and resulting financial requirements, and ultimately, by the alternatives available. And even though some of these alternatives look distinct and separate, your financing strategy will probably encompass a combination of them.

The sources and structures of funding discussed in this chapter are not meant to be all-inclusive, but one point is clear—alternatives to going public do exist.

8

SIMPLIFIED REGISTRATION AND EXEMPTIONS

The SEC continually has been challenged to reduce the regulatory burden placed on smaller registrants and to provide smaller businesses the same access to capital markets as larger enterprises, such as Fortune 500 companies. The end result would be to reduce the initial cost of registration and ongoing expenses of being a public company. In August 1992, the SEC completed the initial phase of Regulation S-B for small business issuers, which included rules that make it easier for small businesses to raise money in the capital markets. The rules simplify the initial and ongoing disclosure and filing requirements for qualifying small businesses and broaden the limits of existing rules related to small offerings. The SEC efforts in this area continued with the adoption of additional small business initiatives in April 1993. The additional guidance provided further transitional disclosure requirements and relaxed the requirements for audited financial statements of acquired businesses. The SEC has stated that they will continue to work with state securities administrators on reducing the regulatory burdens placed on small business issuers.

Regulation S-B sets forth the financial statement and nonfinancial statement disclosure requirements for small business issuer filings under the 1933 Act and the 1934 Act. Regulation S-B is intended to simplify the registration and reporting process by reducing financial and nonfinancial disclosure requirements and publishing these requirements in an all-inclusive regulation.

WHO MAY FILE UNDER REGULATION S-B

To file a registration statement under Regulation S-B, your company must be a United States or Canadian company with annual revenue of less than $25 million in its last fiscal year and voting stock that does not have a public float of $25 million or more. Investment companies are not permitted to use Regulation S-B. Further, if the small business issuer is a majority-owned subsidiary of another company, its parent must also meet the definition of a small business issuer in order for the subsidiary to use Regulation S-B. The public float of a company making an initial public offering of securities is determined based on the number of shares held by nonaffiliates prior to the offering and the estimated public offering price of the securities. Public float for purposes of Regulation S-B is defined as the aggregate market value of the issuer's voting stock held by nonaffiliates.

Once eligible, a company may continue reporting under the small business integrated disclosure system until it exceeds $25 million in revenue for two consecutive fiscal years or $25 million in public float for two consecutive years. However, if a company exceeds the revenue limit in one year, but not the public float limit, and the next year exceeds the public float limit, but not the revenue limit, it will still qualify as a small business issuer. If a company exceeded the limits and was not eligible to file under Regulation S-B, the company must meet the definition of a small business issuer for two consecutive fiscal years before it will be eligible to file under Regulation S-B. The SEC adopted this two-year test to avoid the possibility that temporary changes in the level of revenue or public float would force a small business issuer to prematurely enter or exit the small business disclosure system. Continued eligibility to use the small business reporting system will be determined at the beginning of each fiscal year.

THE REGISTRATION PROCESS

Chapter 5 discusses the registration of initial public offerings utilizing Form S-1. As noted, such a filing is subject to compliance with Regulations S-X and S-K. Regulation S-B simplifies these registration and reporting rules by creating a level of required disclosure that is somewhat less than that required for larger registrants. Some of the requirements under Regulation S-B differ from the requirements under Regulations S-X and S-K.

Financial Statements

Regulation S-B requires an audited balance sheet as of the end of the most recent fiscal year and audited statements of income, cash flows, and changes in shareholders' equity for each of the two years preceding such audited balance sheet, all prepared in accordance with GAAP.

Financial Statement Schedules

Under Regulation S-B, the registrant is not required to include the financial statement schedules required under Regulation S-X. The elimination of the schedules reduces recordkeeping and Annual Report preparation time.

Significant Acquisitions

Regulation S-B requires audited financial statements for significant acquisitions. Significance is defined in terms of the relationship of the target's income and total assets to the registrant, as well as the relationship of the acquisition price to the registrant's total assets. If the highest level of significance exceeds 10 percent but does not exceed 20 percent, one year of audited financial statements is required. If significance exceeds 20 percent, two years of audited financial statements are required. However, where audited financial statements are not readily available, such audited financial statements are automatically waived where the significance of the acquisition does not exceed 20 percent, and the earlier of the two years of audited financial statements are automatically waived where significance of the acquisition does not exceed 40 percent. However, if unaudited financial statements are available they generally must be filed.

Nonfinancial Statement Disclosure Requirements

Certain nonfinancial statement disclosure requirements covered in Regulation S-K, such as executive compensation and description of business, have been simplified and other disclosures, such as selected financial data and supplementary financial information, are no longer required. MD&A disclosure is required for small business issuers that have had revenue in each of their last two fiscal years; other small business issuers would provide business plan information. Executive compensation disclosure rules issued by the SEC in October 1992 are not applicable to, or are phased in for, small business issuers eligible to use Regulation S-B.

Regulation S-B does not preclude small business issuers from registering securities on Forms S-2, S-3, S-4, or S-8 if they otherwise meet the requirements for use of these forms. Amendments to such forms provide that the small business issuer can satisfy the narrative and financial disclosure requirements for Forms S-2, S-3, S-4, or S-8 by complying with the disclosure requirements of Regulation S-B rather than Regulations S-X and S-K.

The new rules also are intended to facilitate registration of debt, preferred stock, common stock, and other securities on one registration statement by no longer requiring the registrant to specify the dollar amount of each class of security to be offered. All issuers eligible to use Form S-3 can now specify an aggregate dollar amount of securities to be offered and the categories of securities that may be involved. Any combination of the disclosed class or category of securities, up to the aggregate dollar amount registered, can be taken off the shelf without preclearance by the SEC.

Appendix E compares the requirements of a registration statement filed on Form S-1 to SB-2.

PERIODIC REPORTING

Regulation S-B created Form 10-KSB as an annual report form and Form 10-QSB as a quarterly report form. Pursuant to Regulation S-B, Form 10-KSB provides for financial and nonfinancial statement disclosures that are more limited than those required in Form 10-K. Form 10-QSB requires essentially the same disclosure and financial information as the current Form 10-Q; however, one difference is that Form 10-QSB does not require a balance sheet as of the preceding fiscal year-end.

OVERVIEW OF EXEMPTIONS FROM REGISTRATION

Securities laws require that an offering of securities be registered unless a specific exemption from registration is available. If no exemptions are available, a company seeking to offer its securities must register them under the 1933 Act by filing the appropriate registration statement under Regulation S-X (such as Form S-1) or Regulation S-B (such as Forms SB-1 or SB-2) and obtaining SEC clearance before selling those securities. A company also must satisfy the securities laws of any state in which securities are offered. It should be noted that registration statements prepared under Regulation S-B may not meet the requirements of securities laws in all states.

Both federal and most state laws provide exemptions from registration in specified circumstances. Note, however, that exemption from registration under federal law does not necessarily result in similar state exemptions. Further, a securities offering is never exempt from the antifraud provisions of the federal securities laws.

The most commonly used exemptions from federal registration requirements are the "private placements" and "limited offering" exemptions provided for by the 1933 Act. Regulations A and D set forth the SEC's rules governing the availability of, and conditions attached to, these exemptions.

Other federal registration exemptions include private placements under Sections 4(2) and 4(6) and intrastate offerings (Rule 147 "safe harbor"). These exemptions and Regulation A have not been as commonly used as Regulation D; however, with the "test the waters" provisions, discussed later, Regulation A offerings take on a different appeal. The specific rules and restrictions applying to each of the federal exemptions are summarized in Appendix D. Your attorneys will advise you on which registration exemption(s) may be available to your company.

Advantages and Disadvantages

Many companies that qualify for an exemption from registration choose to proceed with a registered public offering anyway; but for others, an exempt offering may be an attractive alternative, in particular when you are uncertain as to the extent of public investment interest in your company. In fact, some companies may conclude that, in their circumstances, an exempt offering is the only viable way to raise equity capital. Before deciding, you should weigh the advantages and disadvantages.

On the positive side, an exempt offering is generally less expensive and less time-consuming than a registered public offering. Disclosure and audit requirements for exempt offerings vary, but are generally less extensive than for a registered public offering.

On the negative side, with certain exempt offerings, limits are imposed on the number and qualifications of investors who may purchase the shares and, in some cases, on the amount that may be raised. Restrictions may also be imposed on the subsequent resale of shares, and the lack of a public market for the shares also creates a practical constraint on resale of the shares. Share price may be lower than that obtainable through a registered public offering because of constraints on the number of purchasers and on resale of the shares. Finally, you will not obtain the publicity that results from a public offering and the public image that accrues to a public company.

Prior to a registered public offering, some companies use the exemptions to issue shares to employees, friends, and business associates before the public offering price is determined. (Note however, that this may result in certain constraints when you do go public, as discussed in Chapter 6.)

TESTING THE WATERS

As discussed in Chapter 5, the registration process is an expensive process. The legal and accounting fees, SEC filing fee, NASD filing fee, and underwriter out-of-pocket expenses must be paid even if the offering is unsuccessful. Because the underwriters' discount or commission is based upon total offering proceeds, this cost would not be paid in an unsuccessful registration; however, the underwriters, in some cases, may be entitled to receive compensation for the professional time they incurred.

Historically, the SEC has not permitted solicitation of any kind prior to the filing of the registration statement. If a company is found to have violated this rule, the SEC will typically require the offering be delayed for a sufficient time as to allow the marketplace to cool off, which could damage the timing of the offering. Following the filing of the offering statement, the preliminary offering circular (discussed in Chapter 5) can be utilized to solicit indications of interest; however, at this stage of the process, many of the registration costs have already been incurred.

Under the Regulation A exemption, the SEC will permit companies to "test the waters" for potential public interest in the company prior to the preparation or filing of the offering statement with the SEC. Companies are allowed to test the market through oral presentations, as well as newspaper and media advertisements. All "test the waters" documents and broadcast scripts are required to be submitted to the SEC at the time of their first use. In the case of oral presentations, a copy of the speech or an outline of the presentation should be submitted.

The rules generally do not specify the content of the preoffering material, thus allowing small business issuers to include whatever factual information they deem useful to inform potential investors about the company and its business. However, the presentation would be subject to all of the SEC's antifraud provisions. The regulations state that certain minimum information be included in the presentation materials, including a brief description of the issuer's business, products, and chief executive officer. Further, these materials must include language to make it clear that no money is being solicited by the presentation and that no sales can be made nor money accepted until delivery and qualification of the offering statement, and that indications of interest involve no obligation or commitment of any kind.

If, after "testing the waters," the company decides not to offer securities for sale, then no further filings or notifications to the SEC are required. However, if there is apparent interest, the company may file the Regulation A offering statement either with the SEC's main office or with the appropriate regional office. Once the offering statement is filed with the SEC, the company may no longer distribute or present the "test the waters" materials. In addition, at least 20 calendar days must elapse between the last use of the solicitation of interest document or broadcast and any sale of securities in the Regulation A offering. In the case of a company that determined, based on its "testing the waters," that a potential market exists for an amount in excess of the Regulation A limit, the SEC will permit the "test the waters" material to be deemed exempt under certain conditions if the issuer then files a registration statement. These conditions include allowing 30 calendar days to elapse between the last solicitation of interest (all of which must have been filed with the SEC) and the filing of a registration statement.

COMPARATIVE TABLE

Table 8–1, which follows on pages 136 and 137, highlights the significant provisions and restrictions that apply to small business issuers' registrations on Forms SB-1 and SB-2, and the principal federal registration exemptions. It should be read in conjunction with the discussion in this chapter and Appendix D.

TABLE 8–1.   Comparative Table.

| | Private and Limited Offering Regulation D | | |
	Rule 504	Rule 505	Rule 506
Dollar limit	$1 million in any 12-month period	$5 million in any 12-month period	None
Limit on number of purchasers	No	35 nonaccredited, unlimited accredited	35 nonaccredited,[c] unlimited accredited
Qualification for purchasers	No	No	Nonaccredited must be sophisticated[c]
Qualifications of issuers	Not available for investment companies, blank check companies, or reporting companies[b]	Not available for investment companies or those disqualified by "bad boy" provisions[b]	No
Disclosure requirements[a]	Not specified	Only if one or more nonaccredited purchasers	Only if one or more nonaccredited purchasers
Financial statement requirements	Not specified	Period varies for audited statements	Period varies for audited statements
General solicitation and advertising prohibited	No	Yes	Yes
Resale restrictions	No	Yes	Yes

[a] See Appendix C—Exemptions from Registration for disclosure requirements.
[b] See Appendix F—Glossary of Terms for definitions.
[c] Each nonaccredited investor (or its representative) must have knowledge and experience in financial and business matters and be capable of evaluating the merits and risks of the prospective investment.

TABLE 8–1. *(Continued)*

Private Placements Section 4(6)	Intrastate Offerings Rule 147	Unregistered Public Offerings Regulation A	Small Business Issuers Registration Form SB-1	Small Business Issuers Registration Form SB-2
$5 million	None	$5 million in any 12-month period[d]	$10 million in any 12-month period	None
No	No	No	No	No
All must be accredited	All must be registrants of a single state	No	No	No
No	Must be resident and do business in same state as purchasers	Available for U.S. and Canadian companies only; Not available for reporting companies, blank check companies, investment companies, sale of oil and gas or mineral rights, or those disqualified by "bad boy" provisions	Available for U.S. and Canadian companies with revenue and public float of less than $25 million; Not available for investment companies or subsidiaries whose parent is not qualified to use the form	Available for U.S. and Canadian companies with revenue and public float of less than $25 million; Not available for investment companies or subsidiaries whose parent is not qualified to use the form
Not specified	Not specified	Yes	Yes	Yes
Not specified	Not specified	Two years of unaudited statements	Two years of audited statements	Two years of audited statements
Yes	No	No	No	No
Yes	Yes	Yes[g]	No	No

---

[d] The $5 million limit includes up to $1.5 million for resale of securities by selling shareholders.
[e] No affiliate resales are permitted unless the issuer has had net income from continuing operations in at least one of its last two fiscal years.

APPENDIXES

APPENDIX A

SELECTING A STOCK MARKET*

Not all stock markets are the same. They vary by listing requirements (to begin trading) and maintenance standards (to continue trading) as well as by their rules and regulations governing trading, reporting, and settlement. Stock markets also vary according to market structure and trading mechanisms. These affect market quality in general, which touches all participants, and the services provided, respectively, to issuers, investors, and traders.

There are two types of securities markets operating in the United States. The older, traditional markets, the exchanges—including the national exchanges. The New York Stock Exchange (NYSE) and The American Stock Exchange (Amex) and five regional exchanges—are conducted as auctions on a trading floor where a single specialist assigned to each stock handles orders for a variety of buyers and sellers. A newer market, The Nasdaq Stock Market^SM, has a number of market makers for each stock who either execute or negotiate trades based on firm prices continually broadcast over a computer network.

All U.S. securities markets, whether auction (exchange) or dealer-driven (Nasdaq®), have had an advantage over other

---

*This appendix was written by John T. Wall, Executive Vice President, The Nasdaq Stock Market, Inc. Nasdaq and Nasdaq National Market are registered service marks of The Nasdaq Stock Market, Inc.

markets around the world. A market maker is always involved, whether it is the specialist on an exchange or the multiple market makers of Nasdaq, to offset supply and demand. The distinct advantage of the U.S. exchange markets is that they are not a pure auction environment, as are the European exchange markets, where buy and sell orders interact without any intermediation. The specialist ensures market continuity: someone who is ready and willing to trade at any time.

To ensure this continuity, the specialist is subject to a variety of regulations. In addition, Nasdaq's multiple market makers are induced to provide that continuity by the pressures of competition and market forces, with regulations ensuring the consistency and fairness of that competition.

The strength of the auction market is that there is an effort to have all orders meet in one place: at a specialist's post on the trading floor. Thus, there is a greater chance that a willing buyer and seller will be able to meet at the same price without having to pay anything extra for dealer intermediation. The weakness of the auction market is that it does not have the ability to bring as much capital to bear on stock trading. Because the specialist's capital is limited, there is less willingness to trade in large orders. If a specialist's capital will not cover the order flow, trading halts.

The strengths and weaknesses of a competing, multiple market maker system are the reverse. There is less opportunity for orders to meet without intermediation, but there is much more capital to support trading. Consequently, there is more liquidity and depth for large institutional orders and thus a greater readiness on the part of multiple market makers to trade block orders. Trading never stops for order imbalances.

The choice of market for a company undergoing its initial public offering is usually limited: You may qualify for only certain markets or segments of particular markets. However limited your choice may be; it is wise to choose the best market for your company—one that enhances the attractiveness of your stock to investors and broker/dealers, minimizes your cost of capital, and aids you in fulfilling your responsibilities

as a public company. Definite distinctions can be drawn between the two kinds of U.S. markets in more detail. The older
exchanges tend to feature large Fortune-type 1000 companies
but they also have newer enterprises and IPOs. Nasdaq also
takes well-established companies but is a leader in IPOs. (See
Exhibits A–1 and A–2.)

Exhibit A–1.   Market Distinctions.

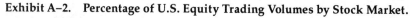

Exhibit A–2.   Percentage of U.S. Equity Trading Volumes by Stock Market.

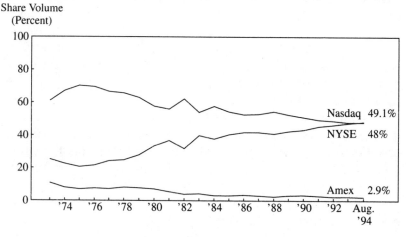

COMPARISON OF MARKET STRUCTURES

Market Platforms

There are both screen-based and floor-based platforms for stock trading. A screen-based market, like Nasdaq, enables participants to trade stocks with each other through a telecommunications network: They access the market on their desktop terminals anywhere they happen to be located while a mainframe computer processes trading information. A traditional floor-based securities market, like an exchange, on the other hand, operates in a specific building, where participants are present to trade stocks. There is no limitation to the number of market participants on a screen-based market. A floor-based market strictly limits the number of participants to those holding "seats." The seats usually are purchased by their firms.

Market Making

Securities markets feature either multiple market makers or a specialist for the trading of a given stock. Screen-based markets enable an unlimited number of *dealers* to make markets in a company's stock, committing to the stock by taking a position in their proprietary accounts. These multiple market makers compete for customer order flow by displaying buy and sell quotations for a guaranteed number of shares broadcast to all market participants over their computer screen. When an order is received, the market maker will immediately purchase for or sell from its own inventory, or the market maker will actively seek the other side of the trade until it is executed.

By contrast, a floor-based exchange assigns all trading activity in a company's stock to one *specialist*, who matches customers orders, trades for its own account, and formulates the public quote for the stock. Like dealers, a specialist also makes markets in a number of different companies' stocks. Unlike a dealer, however, a single specialist has the exclusive right to make a market in a specific company's stock.

Trading Impetus

Securities markets are either quotation-driven or order-driven. Screen-based markets are usually quotation-driven: Dealer bid and ask interest for a guaranteed minimum number of shares is constantly broadcast for other dealers to respond. Continuous trading in a quotation-driven market is therefore more likely. Floor-based exchanges, on the other hand, are order-driven. The specialist responds to incoming buy and sell orders, whose irregularity will influence its ability to make a market in a company's stock. In the absence of orders, the specialist is obligated to display proprietary bids and offers. However, if there is very heavy activity leading to a significant order imbalance, where sell orders outnumber buy orders, or vice versa, and the specialist's proprietary account cannot accommodate the volume, trading is halted.

Trading Environment

Stock trading can occur in either a negotiated or auction environment. A negotiated market is a proactive trading environment that, at minimum, guarantees execution at displayed quotations and number of shares. To conclude a transaction, market makers will trade from their own inventory or actively seek buyers and sellers and will negotiate prices and quantities. Conversely, auction markets react to investor demand. A specialist does not search for buyers and sellers but rather waits for their orders and then fills them by matching them with one another or trading from its own account, if it can.

MARKET QUALITY CHARACTERISTICS

Visibility

Unlike the specialist, who cannot support a company's stock in any way, Nasdaq market makers commit to a company by taking sizable positions in their proprietary accounts, merchandising the stock through their institutional contacts and their own or affiliated retail networks, and maintaining continuous research coverage. These support activities are referred to as "sponsorship." Market makers have a strong incentive to keep a company's stock before investing public and to see it realize its full valuation potential. In addition to their substantial investment in the security, market makers may have the company as an investment banking client.

Depth

Because Nasdaq's structure permits an unlimited number of market makers to trade a company's stock, their aggregate financial position represents substantial available capital to support uninterrupted trading in the stock. Continuous trading capability reassures investors of the stock's marketability, particularly in periods of unusually heavy volume, and helps build shareholder loyalty. Over the past few years, Nasdaq National Market® securities have averaged 11 market makers.

Since an exchange allows only one specialist for each stock traded on its floor, available capital is limited solely to the financial resources of that firm (See Table A–1.) A specialist's available capital to support trading must be allocated among the stocks to which they have an exclusive right to trade. This generally averages 40 stocks. When order imbalances occur and the specialist's account cannot handle the overflow, the specialist declares a halt in the company's stock trading. Though Nasdaq market makers also make markets in a number of stocks, there

TABLE A–1. Total Companies and Market Makers/Specialists by Stock Market (as of June 1994).

	Nasdaq	NYSE	Amex
Number of companies	4812	2471	875
Number of market makers/specialists	509	39	74

are a number of such firms committing capital to any given issue. Thus, Nasdaq only needs to halt trading for material news dissemination, as do the exchanges.

Liquidity

The greater the aggregate financial resources supporting a stock's trading and the more widespread the positions in it, the greater its liquidity: Large blocks can be traded without considerable effect on share price. The consequent reduction in volatility also gives investors confidence in the ownership position they have taken in the company. Wide market swings can distract attention from solid company fundamentals or favorable prospects. Broader participation and competition of multiple market makers drive greater liquidity in a company's stock.

Transparency

Buy and sell quotations that indicate the size and depth of a market in a stock are crucial to the many decisions that companies and investors alike must make. The multiple market makers on Nasdaq constitute the market of a company's stock. All of their bid and offer quotations in a given security are broadcast over the Nasdaq network for all market participants to see. There are no intermediaries.

In comparison, on an exchange, the specialist manages the trading of a company's stock. All bids and offers in a stock are consolidated into the quote of a single specialist. The specialist alone views all of the buy and sell interest in a security and then formulates a public quote that represents the market.

Timing of Execution

Investor confidence in their ownership of a company, so easily influenced by the activity of a stock as much as corporate performance, often depends on ease of trading. The continuous trading capability of a multiple market maker system makes possible immediate execution of orders, particularly for large trades. Market makers will actively seek a matching buyer or seller—or trade out of their own inventory—until the trade is executed, often in a matter of seconds. Though small incoming orders at the prevailing market price and size are also executed immediately on the exchanges, multiple market makers reduce the possibility of order queuing in busy markets.

Entry Requirements

Stringent entry requirements of a stock market distinguish its companies as quality investments. The Nasdaq National Market, the NYSE, and the Amex have comparable entry requirements and maintenance standards for prospective public companies in terms of both financial guidelines and corporate governance standards. (See Table A–2. Another version of this is in Exhibit 6–1.)

Price of Service

Nasdaq's initial (entry) and annual (maintenance) fees for companies are lower than fees among the leading markets, reducing a company's cost in accessing the public markets for capital. (See Table A–3.)

Delisting Requirements

For a company to delist from the NYSE, the company must have the approval of two-thirds of its shareholders and 10 percent may not object. Nasdaq has no delisting requirements.

Cost of Capital

A recent study from Georgetown University* has demonstrated that a company's cost of capital, measured in terms of its

*Reena Aggarwal, "Differences in P/Es and P/Bs of Nasdaq and NYSE Stocks," Georgetown University Working Paper FINC-1377-13-994, September 1994.

TABLE A-2. Entry Requirements on Major Stock Markets.

	Nasdaq National Market		New York Stock Exchange	American Stock Exchange	
	Alternative 1	Alternative 2		Regular	Alternate
Net tangible assets	$4 million	$12 million	$18 million	—	—
Stockholders' equity	—	—	—	$4 million	$4 million
Net income	$400,000[1]	—	—	—	—
Pre-tax income	$750,000[1]	—	$2,500,000[2]	$750,000[1]	—
Public float (shares)	500,000	1 million	1,100,000	500,00 or 1 million[3]	500,000 or 1 million[3]
Market value of public float	$3 million	$15 million	$18 million	$3 million	$15 million
Operating history	—	3 years	—	—	3 years
Minimum bid price	$5	$3	—	$3	$3
Shareholders	800 or 400[3]	400	2,200[4] or 2,000 round lot holders[5]	800 or 400[3]	800 or 400[3]
Market makers	2	2	—	—	—

[1] In latest fiscal year or 2 of last 3 fiscal years.

[2] In addition to $2 million in each of the 2 preceding years or an aggregate pre-tax income for the last 3 years of $6,500,000 with minimum pre-tax earnings of $4,500,000 in the most recent year (all 3 years must be profitable).

[3] If public float is between 0.5 and 1 million shares, 800 shareholders are required. If public float is greater than 1 million shares or more than 0.5 million and average daily volume exceeds 2,000 shares, 400 shareholders are required.

[4] Round lot equals 100 shares or more.

[5] In addition to average monthly trading volume (most recent 6 months) of 100,000 shares.

TABLE A–3. Fees on Major Stock Markets.

Shares (Millions)		Entry Fees[1]			Continuing Annual Fees[2]		
		Nasdaq National Market	NYSE	Amex	Nasdaq National Market[3]	NYSE	Amex
Up to	1	$ 5,000 to 10,000	$51,550	$10,000	$ 5,250	$16,170	$ 6,500
1+ to	2	10,000+ to 15,000	51,550+ to 66,300	15,000	5,750	16,170	7,000
2+ to	3	15,000+ to 20,000	66,300+ to 73,700	20,000	6,250	16,170	7,500
3+ to	4	20,000+ to 25,000	73,700+ to 81,100	22,500	6,750	16,170	8,000
4+ to	5	25,000+ to 30,000	81,100+ to 84,600	25,000	7,250	16,170	8,500
5+ to	6	30,000+ to 32,500	84,600+ to 88,100	27,500	7,750	16,170	9,000
6+ to	7	32,500+ to 35,000	88,100+ to 91,600	30,000	8,250	16,170	9,500
7+ to	8	35,000+ to 37,500	91,600+ to 95,100	32,500	8,750	16,170	10,000
8+ to	9	37,500+ to 40,000	95,100+ to 98,600	35,000	9,250	16,170	10,500
9+ to	10	40,000+ to 42,500	98,600+ to 102,100	37,500	9,750	16,170	11,000
10+ to	11	42,500+ to 45,000	102,100+ to 105,600	42,500	10,250	24,260	11,500
11+ to	12	45,000+ to 47,500	105,600+ to 109,100	42,500	10,750	24,260	12,000
12+ to	13	47,500+ to 50,000	109,100+ to 112,600	42,500	11,250	24,260	12,500
13+ to	14	50,000	112,600+ to 116,100	42,500	11,750	24,260	13,000
14+ to	15	50,000	116,100+ to 119,600	42,500	12,250	24,260	13,500

15+ to 20	50,000	119,600+ to 137,100	50,000	13,250	24,260	14,000[4]
20+ to 25	50,000	137,100+ to 154,600	50,000	13,250	32,340	14,500
25+ to 50	50,000	154,600+ to 242,100	50,000	13,250	32,340+ to 43,140	14,500
50+ to 75	50,000	242,100+ to 329,600	50,000	13,250	48,410+ to 63,890	14,500
75+ to 100	50,000	329,600+ to 417,100	50,000	13,250	63,890+ to 84,640	14,500
100+ to 200	50,000	417,100+ to 767,100	50,000	13,250	84,640+ to 167,640	14,500
Maximum	50,000	[5]	50,000	20,000	500,000	14,500

Source: American Stock Exchange, New York Stock Exchange, and The Nasdaq Stock Market.

[1] The original listing fee for Amex and NYSE is based on the total number of shares listed, including all shares issued and outstanding, as well as shares reserved by the Board of Directors for a specific future issuance. The original fee for Nasdaq National Market is based on total shares outstanding. Fees include one-time initial listing charges of $5,000 for AMEX, $36,800 for NYSE and $5,000 for Nasdaq National Market.

[2] Newly listed Amex and NYSE companies are billed the annual fee on a pro-rata basis at the end of the calendar year in which they are listed. Nasdaq National Market companies are billed the pro-rata annual fee at the end of the month in which they are listed.

[3] For companies with a market capitalization greater than $100 million, an additional fee of $0.025 per $1,000 of the market capitalization above $100 million is applied. Total fee maximums include: $10,000 for companies with 10 million shares or less, $15,000 for companies with 10+ to 20 million shares, and $20,000 for companies with more than 20 million shares.

[4] In excess of 16 million shares outstanding, annual fee is capped at $14,500.

[5] $767,100 plus $.0035 times shares from 200 million to 300 million, plus $.0019 times shares above 300 million.

price/earnings ratio, is lower for Nasdaq companies than for companies whose shares are traded on the NYSE. Over the past 10 years, companies had higher price/earnings multiples on Nasdaq in practically all market-capitalization and industry categories studied. The author attributes this difference to the microstructure of Nasdaq.

Support Services

Nasdaq provides its companies with a variety of information services to aid them in their corporate finance decision-making and investor relations programs. Among these services is a primary contact person qualified to answer questions on the company's stock performance and investor relations matters. Other services include periodic hardcopy reports on company and peer stock activity and an on-line screen-based data system on stock, investor, and market-maker behavior. Specialist firms provide some services to NYSE companies traded by that particular specialist.

Image

Because the exchanges are old stock trading organizations and have older companies, they are associated with the prestige that is associated with age. Investors expect to find established, cyclical companies in basic industries on exchange markets. Nasdaq is known for its innovative, forward-looking growth companies, often in new, evolving industries. Investors anticipate attractive returns with such companies and routinely look to Nasdaq for these opportunities.

CHOOSING AMONG MARKETS

Selecting a securities market in which a company's stock will trade is as important a decision as selecting an investment banker, law firm, and accounting firm. The decision should be given much thought, taking into account the company's responsibilities to its future shareholders and the board of directors' and management's potential ability to fulfill them. Each of the various securities markets may be contacted for additional information.

Stock Markets of the United States

American Stock Exchange, Inc.
86 Trinity Place
New York, NY 10006
(212)306-1640

Boston Stock Exchange, Inc.
One Boston Place
Boston, MA 02108
(617)723-9500 x7206

Chicago Stock Exchange, Inc.
440 S. LaSalle Street
Chicago, IL 60605
(312)663-2618

The Cincinnati Stock Exchange
49 E. Fourth Street, Suite 205
Cincinnati, OH 45202
(312)786-8803

The Nasdaq Stock Market, Inc.
1735 K Street, NW
Washington, DC 20006-1506
(202)728-8840

New York Stock Exchange, Inc.
11 Wall Street
New York, NY 10005
(212)656-2065

Pacific Stock Exchange, Inc.
301 Pine Street
San Francisco, CA 94104
(415)393-4198

Philadelphia Stock Exchange, Inc.
Philadelphia Stock Exchange Building
1900 Market Street
Philadelphia, PA 19103
(215)496-5200

BOARD OF DIRECTORS

SELECTING THE BOARD OF DIRECTORS

When your company becomes public, the board of directors should begin to play a larger role in policy decisions and should include outside representatives who would be acceptable to the investing public. Investors view the composition of the board of directors as an important factor in evaluating a company. Outside directors (i.e., other than management and major shareholders) bring specialized expertise and an independent perspective to the boards of both private and public companies. Your company should consider inviting individuals with proven, relevant expertise to serve as directors. For example, chief executive officers or other executives of other companies may bring operations expertise; bankers may be able to provide you with financial advice; attorneys, accountants, and other professionals could bring legal and financial expertise; and academics might be invited for their recommendations on technical or operational matters. Outside board members not only will help strengthen the management of your company by serving on the board and its committees, but also enhance its credibility with the investment community.

Size

As with any group, a large board allows for the expertise and breadth of experience of its many members. This, however, must be weighed against the disadvantage that a larger group may be unwieldy and therefore not be able to function as effectively. The average size of the board of directors varies according to industry group, asset size, and sales volume. According to the American Bar Association's *Corporate Director's Guidebook*, complex corporations tend to have larger boards, averaging about fifteen members, while smaller industrial concerns average eight or nine members. This is consistent with the notion that relatively smaller boards provide an opportunity for board members to become more involved in discussions and deliberations, which is viewed as positive. Corporations that have larger boards tend to utilize committees for much of their work, which permits a more manageable operating size.

In determining the appropriate number of board members, many companies look to the complexity of the company's operations, the number of issues that either require board involvement or that would benefit from the board's involvement, the size of their competitors' board, and the cost of obtaining and retaining highly qualified board members.

Term

There are no specific laws or regulations that dictate the length of board member service or the frequency regarding reelection or replacement of board members. Some companies elect their entire board on an annual basis, however, minimal turnover from such annual proceedings is expected. Other companies, concerned both with continuity and protection against unsolicited offers, will establish longer terms for board members (e.g., three to five years) and stagger the elections so that only a percentage of the board will stand for election in a given year. Some companies have established their own rules regarding the maximum number of terms a member may serve and some have established a mandatory retirement age for board members.

Basic Duties and Responsibilities

The basic duty of a corporate director is to advance the interests of the corporation. A director is often said to be performing this duty by demonstrating behavior that can be described as diligent and loyal. While these concepts may appear obvious, it is important that directors understand them. Failure to understand the responsibilities of directorship can lead to liability for both the director and the corporation.

Diligence refers to the importance of directors to act in good faith, with the care that an ordinarily prudent person in a like position would exercise, and in a manner believed to be in the best interests of the corporation. Diligence includes such important attributes as consistently attending board meetings and taking the time to ensure that one is fully informed by obtaining and reviewing all pertinent information needed to make an informed decision before the meetings occur. In doing so, directors may rely on the reports of experts such as independent accountants or the corporation's legal counsel.

Loyalty requires that directors act in the interest of the corporation's shareholders and not in the director's own interest or in the interest of another person or organization. Directors should remain alert for any issue that may be construed as conflicting with the best interests of the corporation, and generally should recuse themselves from voting on matters that could involve a conflict of interest.

Directors should be responsive to shareholders in that their primary role is in overseeing the activities of management. After the IPO, the company will have a significant responsibility to its new shareholders.

Independent Directors

The board of directors of a public company (or one that is about to go public) should be organized to encourage and demonstrate the board's function as an independent observer and evaluator of the company's affairs and performance.

The composition of the board will be a major factor in determining the group's effectiveness in promoting the objectives of the corporation. Boards are usually comprised of both management and independent directors. A management director is one whose primary duty is as an employee (typically a senior executive) of the corporation. While these members are important because of their expertise in running the company and their day-to-day familiarity with its operations, boards are increasingly comprised primarily of independent directors. An independent director is one who is not an officer or employee of the company.

Outside board members not only will help strengthen the management of your company by serving on the board and its committees, but also enhance its credibility with the investment community. The independent director is valued because of his or her increased ability to be objective about the company's affairs. Boards comprised of members who simply "rubber stamp" the recommendations of management are prime targets for shareholder lawsuits. A strong board will be perceived positively by the investment community and will serve to strengthen the company as it begins the process of going public.

COMMITTEES OF THE BOARD

Many public companies have found the committee structure to be the most efficient and effective way for their boards to function successfully. The committee approach is especially useful for outside directors who have extensive commitments elsewhere. In addition, the committee structure allows independent directors to specialize and cultivate greater depth of knowledge about specific areas, ranging from financial reporting and internal financial controls to management selection and compensation, thus enhancing their ability to make critical board decisions.

When analyzing committee composition, the role of the independent director becomes increasingly evident. On most committees, the majority of members are independent directors.

The number and size of the various board committees varies among industry groups and companies within those groups. As with the issue of the size of the board itself, the primary advantage to large committees is the broader experience base represented by the members. The disadvantage is that larger committees may become unmanageable and make it difficult for the chairman to keep the committee meetings focused. Each company must determine the appropriate size for its unique circumstance. A discussion of the activities and composition of the more common committees follows.

Audit Committee

Since first recommended by the New York Stock Exchange in 1939, the audit committee has emerged as the most prevalent board committee. Today the NYSE, the American Stock Exchange, and the NASD all require audit committees for their listed companies. The NYSE requires the committee to be comprised entirely of independent directors, while the Amex and NASD require that a majority of the members be independent.

While the overall duties of an audit committee may be relatively similar from company to company, style and methods of operation need not be. Rather, they should be closely tailored to the objectives, needs, and circumstances of the organization the committee is designed to serve. The background and experience of directors, their depth of knowledge of the company's financial position, and the specialized industry regulatory requirements are key factors that should determine the nature and scope of an audit committee's activities.

Typically, the audit committee is established through a formal board resolution. The audit committee must distinguish its oversight responsibility from involvement in the day-to-day management of the company and the conduct of the audit. The committee must not be considered an adversary of management; rather it is part of the corporation's governance and oversight process. A sample audit committee charter is provided in Exhibit B–1.

The most important key to success for an audit committee is effective communication—among the committee and management, the full board, the internal auditors, and the independent auditors.

Although the size of audit committees varies—the Treadway Commission suggests at least three members—each member

Exhibit B–1.   Sample Audit Committee Charter.

ORGANIZATION

There shall be a committee of the board of directors to be known as the audit committee. The audit committee shall be composed of directors who are independent of the management of the corporation and are free of any relationship that, in the opinion of the board of directors, would interfere with their exercise of independent judgment as a committee member.

STATEMENT OF POLICY

The audit committee shall provide assistance to the corporate directors in fulfilling their responsibility to the shareholders, potential shareholders, and investment community relating to corporate accounting, reporting practices of the corporation, and the quality and integrity of the financial reports of the corporation. In so doing, it is the responsibility of the audit committee to maintain free and open means of communication among the directors, the independent auditors, the internal auditors, and the financial management of the corporation.

RESPONSIBILITIES

In carrying out its responsibilities, the audit committee believes its policies and procedures should remain flexible, in order to best react to changing conditions and ensure to the directors and shareholders that the corporate accounting and reporting practices of the corporation are in accordance with all requirements and are of the highest quality.

In carrying out these responsibilities, the audit committee will:

- Review and recommend to the directors the independent auditors to be selected to audit the financial statements of the corporation and its divisions and subsidiaries.

- Meet with the independent auditors and financial management of the corporation to review the scope of the proposed audit for the current year and the audit procedures to be utilized, and at the conclusion thereof review such audit, including any comments or recommendations of the independent auditors.

- Review with the independent auditors, the company's internal auditor, and financial and accounting personnel, the adequacy and effectiveness of the accounting and financial controls of the corporation, and elicit any recommendations for the improvement of such internal control procedures or particular areas where new or more detailed controls or procedures are desirable. Particular emphasis should be given to the adequacy of such internal controls to expose any payments, transactions, or procedures that might be deemed illegal or otherwise improper. Further, the committee periodically should review company policy statements to determine their adherence to the code of conduct.

- Review the internal audit function of the corporation including the independence and authority of its reporting obligations, the proposed audit plans for the coming year, and the coordination of such plans with the independent auditors.

- Receive prior to each meeting, a summary of findings from completed internal audits and a progress report on the proposed internal audit plan, with explanations for any deviations from the original plan.

- Review the financial statements contained in the annual report to shareholders with management and the independent auditors to determine that the independent auditors are satisfied with the disclosure and content of the financial statements to be presented to the shareholders. Any changes in accounting principles should be reviewed.

- Provide sufficient opportunity for the internal and independent auditors to meet with the members of the audit committee without members of management present. Among the items to be discussed in these meetings are the independent auditors' evaluation of the corporation's financial, accounting, and auditing personnel, and the cooperation that the independent auditors received during the course of the audit.

- Review accounting and financial human resources and succession planning within the company.

- Submit the minutes of all meetings of the audit committee to, or discuss the matters discussed at each committee meeting with, the board of directors.

- Investigate any matter brought to its attention within the scope of its duties, with the power to retain outside counsel for this purpose, if, in its judgment, that is appropriate.

should be an active participant in committee activities. Several research studies show that three to five members is fairly standard.

Typically, audit committee charters require that only outside directors be members, which has been encouraged by most research studies and regulatory agencies. Most important is that members be committed to the task and have adequate time to devote to the committee's work.

The responsibilities of the audit committee include oversight over the financial reporting process, the work of internal audit, and the work of the independent auditors.

The Financial Reporting Process

Overseeing the financial reporting process is one of the most important—and most difficult—responsibilities of an audit committee member. To effectively perform this function, the audit committee member needs to understand the company's business and industry and attendant risks.

One of the key elements of an effective financial reporting process is the establishment and maintenance of an effective control environment. An effective control environment minimizes the risk of loss from errors and irregularities, and assures that the confidentiality of information and continuity of operations are maintained. Audit committee members help to set the tone for a proper control environment.

Another important component of the financial reporting process is the reporting of quarterly financial information. Quarterly financial information is heavily relied on by users of financial statements, particularly for public companies. Although management extensively analyzes interim financial information, quarterly financial statements generally include more estimates and judgments than annual financial statements.

The audit committee should be briefed by management, and possibly the internal and independent auditors, on how management develops and summarizes quarterly financial information, the extent to which internal audit is involved in the process, whether the independent auditors have performed any review procedures on the information, and whether those review procedures were performed before or after the information was issued.

Fraudulent financial reporting continues to receive increasing attention in the financial press. What exactly is fraudulent financial reporting, and what can an audit committee do about it? The fraudulent financial reporting we read about differs from theft or embezzlement. Often the intent is to alter the financial statements to reflect other than the facts. Fraudulent financial reporting may involve the misapplication of accounting principles, inappropriate valuations, or outright misrepresentation of facts. Typically, there is no actual diversion of corporate assets. It often is difficult to distinguish fraudulent financial reporting from unintentional errors, because it is often impossible to determine management's intent.

The audit committee is not the "cop on the beat" in these situations, but it can play an important role. Most situations involving fraudulent financial reporting reflect one or more warning signals long before a situation is detected and, in many instances, long before it occurs. Sometimes the audit committee might be in a position to spot these "red flags."

The Internal Audit Function

The internal audit function is a valuable resource. In addition to providing assurances to the audit committee about the adequacy of the system of internal control and participating in the annual independent audit, the internal audit function can help the audit committee by evaluating compliance with corporate policy (e.g., reviewing compliance with the code of conduct or policies relating to capital expenditures and officers' expenses) and by performing audits for operating efficiencies (e.g., looking for ways to make a distribution center more efficient). In some companies, the internal audit function helps conduct special projects the committee has assumed responsibility for, such as special investigations for illegal payments or potential fraud.

The audit committee should periodically review the mission statement of the internal audit function and evaluate it against the committee's expectations and needs. This review should help assure internal audit resources are used to the best advantage.

As it does with the independent auditors, the audit committee should review the planned scope of the internal auditors' work, the results of their work, and management's actions regarding their recommendations.

Independent Auditors

One of the primary responsibilities of the audit committee is to oversee the financial reporting process. Through their involvement, the independent auditors are in a position to provide an objective assessment of this process, the audit committee should maintain open lines of communication with the independent auditors. Most notably, the audit committee should inquire about the proposed audit scope and approach, any suggestions or recommendations management receives from the independent auditors, and the results of the annual audit.

Because management works most closely with the independent auditors, they are in a better position to evaluate the level and quality of services provided. As such, they usually make a proposal on the appointment of the independent auditors to the audit committee. The audit committee reviews this proposal and then recommends the firm to the board of directors. The board of directors is responsible for actually appointing the independent auditors, which is often subject to ratification by the shareholders.

Along with the responsibility of overseeing the financial reporting process, another responsibility of the audit committee is to determine that sufficient audit coverage is provided by the internal and independent auditors.

The audit committee's role as it relates to the independent auditors is to determine that the scope of their services is appropriate based on the needs of the company. Although the audit committee might inquire as to the independent auditor's fees and total audit costs (internal and independent auditors), the audit committee's primary concern is to ensure that management has not inadvertently restricted the audit scope (independent or internal) in its desire to control costs. It remains management's responsibility to negotiate fees with the independent auditors.

Compensation Committee

Executive compensation recently has become one of the most hotly debated issues of corporate governance. The debate centers around the compensation that is paid to the CEO and other members of senior management, and the question of whether the often lucrative salary and benefits package is justified by the performance of the executive and the corporation.

While a privately held company need not disclose the compensation of its key executives, a public company must disclose the compensation of its CEO and its other four most highly compensated executive officers. A responsible compensation committee of the board of directors can aid the board in assessing the performance and resulting compensation of key executives.

Strategically, the compensation committee should consider how the achievement of the overall goals and objectives of the corporation can be aided through adoption of an appropriate compensation philosophy and an effective compensation program. This is an important issue for a company about to go public, because compensation often plays an important role in attracting and retaining management talent.

Administratively, the compensation committee reviews salary progression, bonus allocations, stock awards, and the awards of supplemental benefits and perquisites for key executives and compares them against the compensation objectives and overall performance of the company. Generally, the compensation committee is concerned only with the compensation levels of senior executives. In order to be an effective tool for corporate governance on behalf of the shareholders, the committee should be composed of independent directors.

While not required in a registration statement, the SEC requires that a report to shareholders by the members of the compensation committee (or other group functioning in that capacity) be included in a proxy or other information statement relating to an annual meeting. The report should discuss the company's compensation policies for executive officers and the committee's basis for determining the compensation of the CEO and certain other highly compensated employees for the past year.

Just as the audit committee has access to outside advisors to determine the integrity of the firm's financial controls, the compensation committee may seek assistance from compensation consultants. Specialists can advise them as to the competitiveness of the company's compensation structure within the same industry, as well as with companies of similar size in different industries. Many compensation committees have responded to the requirement of providing a detailed compensation committee report by retaining consultants to assist in the determination of compensation, as well as in the drafting of the report.

Executive Committee

Historically, the executive committee has served as a key link between the board and management, especially during periods between board meetings. The committee usually is granted broad powers to assure that important matters that cannot wait until the next scheduled meeting receive timely attention. Executive committees also can help the full board function more efficiently, particularly when the board is large. It may serve as a sounding board for general management problems involving matters that affect the corporation as a whole.

Companies often assign retired chief executive officers or other senior members of management to serve on this committee, as their experience in managing the company is often valuable. The chairs of other key board committees often serve as members of the executive committee, as well. Given its orientation toward management issues, it is not surprising to find the greatest percentage of management directors sitting on the executive committee.

Finance Committee

In this era of acquisitions, mergers, and general financial uncertainty, the finance committee's role is growing more critical, particularly in larger companies. This committee is most likely to be present in larger corporations with more complex financial structures.

The finance committee is primarily involved with financial decisions and planning. Its responsibilities include:

- Staying informed on a timely basis about the company's financial status.
- Evaluating the financial information it receives and developing conclusions as to any plan of action needed.
- Advising corporate management and the full board on financial matters. Although usually not empowered to act on its own, in some instances, the finance committee is authorized to make decisions on behalf of the full board during periods between board meetings.

Nominating Committee

As corporate America finds it increasingly difficult to find qualified candidates willing to serve on the board of directors, the job of the nominating committee becomes ever more critical to ensure the long-term strength of the board. For a company deciding to go public, such a committee would be given the responsibility of thoroughly searching and screening candidates for initial board positions or board vacancies. To achieve this, the nominating committee must consider the broader issues of the composition and organization of the board, including committee assignments and individual board membership. Additionally, the nominating committee evaluates the board itself and its members and reviews the company's management succession planning.

Candidates recommended to the nominating committee for board membership often have had prior contact with the chief executive officer and other board members. In addition, nominating committees are increasingly relying on outside consultants to fulfill their tasks. These advisors generally help screen candidates to provide greater assurance of independence in candidate selection—independence in fact and in appearance.

In general, all nominees recommended by the committee stand for election by the corporation's shareholders. In some instances, though, boards have the authority to elect a director to fill a vacancy for the remainder of a term.

BOARD COMPENSATION

To attract and retain qualified and talented directors, corporations in a competitive environment are offering independent directors increasingly attractive compensation and benefits packages. Furthermore, as the time pressures and responsibilities placed upon directors increase, we can expect a greater focus on compensation in the coming years.

Virtually all public companies compensate their independent directors for the time spent on board activities, with the most popular payment method being a combination of an annual retainer and a per meeting fee. Traditionally, corporations pay management directors only as employees. They generally do not award additional compensation for their work on the board of directors.

Many executives and shareholders believe the compensation of directors, like that of operating management, should be more closely tied to the financial well-being of the company. Companies with this philosophy often provide some form of stock-based compensation to their directors. A substantial majority of independent directors who serve on board committees receive additional compensation for those efforts. In contrast, management directors are rarely paid for committee service. The most prevalent method of compensating independent directors for committee service is by meeting fee only, although some corporations choose to pay an annual retainer or combination of the two methods. Typically, the committee chair receives additional compensation.

A number of companies offer retirement plans to their outside directors. The majority of the companies offering retirement plans base eligibility for participation on both the director's specified ages and years of service on the board.

Many public companies offer their outside directors some form of a deferred compensation plan, and the most common scenario is for directors to defer their compensation until retirement. These plans tend to be popular as they may allow the deferral of income that is not subject to the limits imposed by the Employee Retirement Income Security Act (ERISA) and the Tax Equity and Fiscal Responsibility Act (TEFRA). These acts limit the amount of retirement income that can be provided by the director's regular employer.

Some corporations permit independent directors and certain management directors to participate in a charitable awards program. Generally, these programs allow qualified participants to designate a contribution to be made by the corporation at a future date in time. One such program takes the form of a substantial contribution to be made by the corporation to a designated charitable organization upon a director's death. The funding for such a contribution is obtained through the purchase by the corporation of a whole-life insurance policy, the premiums for which are paid by the corporation.

ACCOUNTING AND REPORTING ISSUES ASSOCIATED WITH AN INITIAL PUBLIC OFFERING

Companies entering the public markets for the first time face many new and unique challenges, including accounting and reporting requirements they never faced as a private company. The accounting and reporting issues are often complex, due to the additional requirements imposed by the securities laws, or as a result of differences when compared to traditional GAAP. The purpose of this appendix is to highlight many of the accounting and reporting issues companies preparing for an IPO should be familiar with, and to provide guidance in addressing them.

OVERVIEW OF SEC RULES AND REGULATIONS

The SEC requirements of financial reporting and disclosure are set forth in numerous rules and regulations that can take many forms. The discussion that follows provides a brief overview of the different sources of authoritative guidance that companies considering an initial public offering should be familiar with.

Most of the SEC requirements for financial statements and the rules as to their form and content are contained in Regulation S-X. Regulation S-X applies to filings under the 1933 Act, the 1934 Act, the Public Utility Holding Company Act of 1935, and the Investment Company Act of 1940. Financial statement requirements for registrants who meet the requirements and file as a small business issuer under Regulation S-B may be found in Item 310 of that Regulation. S-B filers are not subject to the requirements of Regulation S-X.

Regulation S-X

To understand the instructions for financial statements in Regulation S-X, the precise meanings of the terms that are used must be known. Many of these terms are defined in Rule 1-02 of Regulation S-X, Regulation C of the 1933 Act, and Regulation 12B of the General Rules and Regulations under the 1934 Act.

Regulation S-X requires financial statement disclosures beyond those required by GAAP. These additional disclosures may be required in footnotes, schedules, separate financial statements, or summarized financial information. The SEC considers these disclosures necessary for investors, security analysts, and other users of the financial statements.

Normally, Regulation S-X should be strictly adhered to; however, when more informative statements can be produced by modifying provisions of Regulation S-X, a common sense approach can be considered. Such modifications should generally be cleared with the SEC staff in advance of filing.

Regulation S-X Rule 4-01(a) states that "The information required with respect to any statement shall be furnished as a minimum requirement to which shall be added such further material information as is necessary to make the required statements, in the light of the circumstances under which they are made, not misleading." It is important to note that the SEC regards Regulation S-X as being only a minimum standard.

When there have been major changes in Regulation S-X or other SEC rules or regulations, the financial statements presented for prior years, as well as the current year, generally should conform to the new rules or regulations.

Regulation S-B

Regulation S-B reduces the periods for which financial statements are required in annual reports and registration statements (one balance sheet and two statements of income, cash flows, and changes in stockholders' equity), eliminates Regulation S-X footnote disclosures that are not required by GAAP, and reduces the extent of nonfinancial statement disclosures required in registration statements and periodic reports.

Financial Reporting Releases

The SEC publishes rules on accounting and financial reporting matters. These rules are contained in Financial Reporting Releases (FRRs) and have the same authority as Regulation S-X.

New rules or amendments of existing rules pertaining to accounting, financial reporting, and auditing matters in Regulations S-X and S-K, and in SEC registration and reporting forms are set forth in FRRs.

Staff Accounting Bulletins

Staff Accounting Bulletins (SABs) are used to disseminate administrative interpretations and practices used by the staff of the SEC. They are distinguishable from FRRs in that the statements are not rules or interpretations of the SEC nor are they published as bearing the SEC's official approval; they represent interpretations and practices followed by the Division of Corporation Finance and the Office of the Chief Accountant in administering the disclosure requirements of the federal securities laws.

While SABs do not have the same authority as FRRs and other SEC rules, administrative positions taken by the SEC staff can exert significant influence on the form and content of financial statements. The staff has shown little willingness to accept departures from SABs. Further, the SEC staff believes that SABs should be applied in analogous circumstances (SAB Topic 6.G).

SEC Guides

From time to time, the SEC has issued industry guides that also must be considered in the preparation of registration statements and periodic reports. The guides that are presently effective for registration statements under the 1933 Act are:

- Guide 1—Disclosure by electric and gas utilities
- Guide 2—Disclosure of oil and gas operations
- Guide 3—Statistical disclosure by bank holding companies
- Guide 4—Prospectuses relating to interests in oil and gas programs
- Guide 5—Preparation of registration statements relating to interests in real estate limited partnerships
- Guide 6—Disclosures concerning unpaid claims and claim adjustment expenses of property-casualty insurance underwriters
- Guide 7—Description of property by issuers engaged or to be engaged in significant mining operations

Guides 1, 2, 3, and 6 are also applicable to periodic reports; Guide 6 under the 1933 Act is the same as Guide 4 under the 1934 Act. Guides are not rules of the SEC nor are they published as having the SEC's official approval. They represent policies and practices followed by the Division of Corporation Finance— and, in some instances, the Office of the Chief Accountant—in administering the disclosure requirements of the federal securities laws.

Other SEC Rules and Regulations

The SEC publishes General Rules and Regulations under each of the Acts that it administers. These rules are important when dealing with accounting and reporting issues because they prescribe numbers of copies, modes of printing, and physical presentation of documents to be filed. They also define terms and contain other data that often directly or indirectly affect financial statements. For instance, various rules deal with incorporation by reference and Rule 12b-25 covers notification procedures when documents are not filed timely.

SEC Staff Positions

Consideration should be given to SEC staff positions on accounting or disclosure issues that are less formal and do not carry the same authoritative stature of SABs. SEC staff positions are communicated to registrants and their auditors through various sources including: speeches given by SEC Commissioners or staff; no-action letters in response to registrant inquiries; informal discussions with the SEC staff; SEC staff training materials; and SEC staff comment letters on registrant filings.

Like SABs, SEC staff positions are not rules or interpretations of the SEC nor do they bear the SEC's official approval. They represent interpretations and practices followed by the Division of Corporation Finance and the Office of the Chief Accountants in administering the accounting and disclosure requirements of the federal securities laws.

ACCOUNTING ISSUES

The following is a brief summary of certain accounting issues that relate primarily to new public companies. The purpose of this discussion is to assist companies in identifying accounting issues that may be relevant when considering an IPO. If any of these accounting issues appear to apply to your company, your accounting professionals should be consulted during the process of deciding whether or not to pursue an IPO.

Past or Probable Future Business Combinations

Rule 3-05 of Regulation S-X describes the SEC's requirements for registrants to provide audited financial statements of a business acquired or to be acquired, including acquisition of an interest in a business accounted for under the equity method. An overview of the financial statement requirements of Rule 3-05 is included in Appendix C–1.

It is important to note that the SEC staff's interpretation of what is a business is rather broad. In several cases, the SEC has overruled registrants who believed that separate financial statements were not required because the purchase of a portion of another company's assets did not constitute the acquisition of a business. In one instance, the SEC staff considered the assets constituting a particular production process to be a "business" because the acquiring company continued to produce the predecessor's product, even though production was moved to a different location and most prior employees and management were not retained.

Rule 11-01(d) of Regulation S-X describes the SEC's interpretation of what constitutes a business. According to the SEC, each situation must ". . . be evaluated in light of the facts and circumstances involved and whether there is sufficient continuity of the acquired entity's operations prior to and after the transactions so that disclosure of prior financial information is material to an understanding of future operations." While a separate company, subsidiary, or division is usually a business, a lesser component of an entity also may be a business. The SEC believes the following should be considered in making the evaluation:

- Whether the nature of the revenue-producing activity of the component will remain generally the same after the transaction as before the transaction; or

- Whether any of the following attributes remain with the component after the transaction:
  - Physical facilities
  - Employee base
  - Market distribution system
  - Sales force

APPENDIX C–1. Overview of Rule 3-05 Requirements.

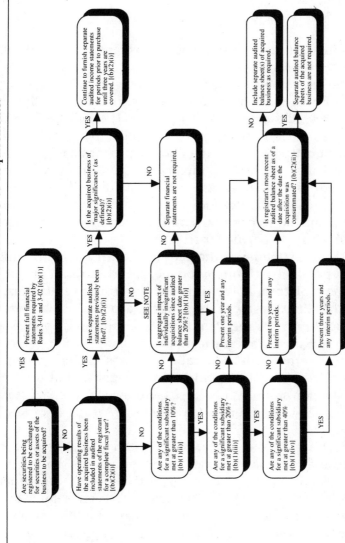

Note: For initial public offerings, the SEC requires that audited financial statements of the registrant and/or predecessors so that 90% in the latest year, 80% in preceding year, and 60% in second preceding year are audited.

* The requirement to provide financial statements of individually insignificant acquired businesses is applicable only to transactional filings. (e.g. Form S-3) or to Forms 8-K which will be incorporated by reference into a transactional filings.

— Customer base
— Operating rights
— Production techniques
— Trade names.

These guidelines are not all-inclusive, so management must use judgment in this area.

Traditionally, public companies have been allowed to use pro forma information when making the significance tests that are needed. The SEC staff, in SAB 80 (Topic 1.J), *Application of Rule 3-05 in Initial Public Offerings,* provided relief to companies that are going public by allowing them to use pro forma information in their calculations if the company was built through the aggregation of discrete businesses that remain substantially intact after the acquisition. Before SAB 80 many private companies have been unable to comply with the literal requirements of Rule 3-05 when preparing for an IPO.

The SEC staff believes the acquired entity's significance in this type of situation may be measured in relation to the size of the registrant at the time the registration statement is filed, rather than its size at the time the acquisition was made. Thus, for a first-time registrant, the SEC staff will apply Regulation S-X, Rule 3-05 significance tests against the pro forma financial statements of the total of the entities, including entities to be acquired, that comprise the registrant at the time the registration statement is filed. Guidance for preparing pro forma financial statements is provided in Article 11 of Regulation S-X.

In brief, SAB 80 requires that not less than three, two, and one year(s) of audited financial statements for not less than 60 percent, 80 percent, and 90 percent, respectively, of the constituent businesses that will comprise the registrant on an ongoing basis be included in an IPO registration statement. Additional details of the requirement, and an example of its application, are included in SAB 80.

Manditorily Redeemable Equity Securities

Manditorily redeemable preferred stocks (RPS) are those equity securities that are either subject to mandatory redemption requirements or whose redemption is outside the control of the issuer. These shares are often referred to as "mezzanine" capital because they are to be reported on the balance sheet between liabilities and stockholders' equity. Rule 5-02 of Regulation S-X, which specifically requires that they not be shown under a general stockholders' equity heading, has been interpreted to apply *to any equity security* with similar redemption characteristics. RPS may not be presented in a total that includes nonredeemable preferred stock, common stock, and other stockholders' equity.

Convertible Debt and Redeemable Preferred Stock

The major issue involving changes in capital structure involves whether there should be retroactive restatement of the balance sheet for all periods presented when there is a change in capitalization. Examples include debt and RPS that converts to common stock, and changes in capital structure resulting from a change in legal form (partnership or corporation) or tax status (Subchapter S or Chapter C companies). In general, the SEC staff will object to a retroactive restatement of the financial statements.

The primary issue involving RPS relating to an IPO involves the historical financial statement presentation of RPS that converts to common stock on the effective date of the IPO. The RPS should be shown in the mezzanine until the date the conversion occurs. Upon conversion, prior period financial statements should not be restated to present the RPS as common stock nor to reclassify the RPS into permanent equity.

Generally, the historical balance sheet or statement of operations should not be revised to reflect conversions or term modifications of outstanding RPS that become effective after the last balance sheet date presented in the filing. Pro forma data presented with the historical statements would generally be required if the conversion or modifications have a dilutive effect.

Changes in Capitalization

Material changes in the capitalization of a registrant that will be effected coincident with the closing of the IPO are to be presented in a separate pro forma balance sheet column beside the historical balance sheet in the primary financial statements. The pro forma column should reflect only the change in capitalization as if it occurred on the latest balance sheet date included in the filing.

In addition to historical earnings per share, registrants should present pro forma EPS data on the face of the statement of operations, giving effect to the change in capitalization as of the beginning of the latest fiscal year carried forward through the most recent interim period presented in the filing. In cases where the registrant can demonstrate that pro forma EPS for earlier periods would be meaningful and factually supportable, the SEC staff will not object. Pro forma data should be clearly labeled, and a note to the financial statements should explain the basis of presentation.

Such financial statement disclosures are not required for changes in capitalization that do not affect equity (such as debt refundings and retirements). Conversions of nonredeemable preferred stock to common stock effected at or prior to the effective date may not be shown on a retroactive basis in the historical financial statements. If such conversions will take place only at the closing of the IPO, the pro forma presentation just discussed would be appropriate.

Historical Financial Statements
Not Indicative of the Ongoing Entity

In some instances, the historical financial statements are not indicative of the ongoing entity (e.g., tax or other cost sharing agreements will be terminated or revised). In these situations, the registration statement should include pro forma income statements, prepared in accordance with Article 11 of Regulation S-X (most recent fiscal year and interim period), which reflect the impact of terminated or revised cost sharing agreements and other significant changes.

Cash Dividends Declared
Subsequent to the Balance Sheet Date

When cash dividends are declared by the subsidiary subsequent to the date of the latest balance sheet included in a registration statement, the staff requires that such dividends be reflected in a pro forma balance sheet included alongside the historical balance sheet.

Distribution to Owners at or Prior to Closing of an IPO

If a distribution will be paid to current owners of the company out of the proceeds of the IPO, or if dividends paid in the year prior to the IPO exceeded earnings during that period, the SEC staff has indicated that historical earnings per share (EPS) should be deleted and pro forma EPS should be disclosed. Pro forma EPS should give effect to the number of shares whose proceeds would be required to pay the dividend (SAB Topic 1.B).

Additionally, any significant distribution or planned distribution to owners that is not reflected in the historical balance sheet requires the presentation of a pro forma balance sheet alongside the historical balance sheet. The pro forma balance sheet should reflect the distribution, but should not reflect any proceeds from the offering.

Escrowed Shares

In order to facilitate an initial public offering by some companies, underwriters have requested that some or all shareholders (some or all of whom may be employees) of the privately held company place a portion of their shares in an escrow account. The escrowed shares generally are legally outstanding and may continue to have voting and dividend rights. The shares are released from escrow based on the attainment of certain performance measures by the company in subsequent periods, such as specified earnings or market price levels. If the levels are not achieved, the escrow shares are returned to the company and canceled.

Even though these shares are legally outstanding and are reported as such on the face of the balance sheet, the SEC staff considers the placement of shares in escrow to be a recapitalization similar to a reverse stock split. The agreement to release the shares upon the achievement of certain criteria is presumed by the staff to be a separate compensatory arrangement between the registrant and the promoters. Accordingly, the fair value of the shares at the time the shares are released from escrow is recognized as a charge to income in that period. However, this presumption can be overcome for specific shareholders if they (1) have not held and will not hold positions that could affect the financial results of the company (e.g., employee, officer, director, consultant, contractor) and (2) have been and will continue to be shareholders that have no relationship with the company other than as common shareholders.

Issuances of Shares Prior to the IPO

The SEC staff requires registrants to treat issuances shares of stock, options, or warrants in the twelve months preceding an IPO as if they were outstanding for all periods presented in computing earnings per share. The staff will accept the use of the Treasury stock method described in APB Opinion 15, *Earnings per Share,* in measuring dilution except that the effect of the additional securities should be included in earnings per share even if the effect is anti-dilutive. (See SAB Topic 4.D.)

EXEMPTIONS FROM REGISTRATION

PRIVATE AND LIMITED OFFERINGS—REGULATION D

The SEC adopted Regulation D in 1982 in an effort to make the capital markets more accessible for small businesses. Regulation D allows companies to reduce the burdensome, costly registration requirements applicable to small and private offerings of securities.

Certain portions of Regulation D represent a "nonexclusive safe harbor" under Section 4(2) of the 1933 Act. In other words, a company may be able to qualify for exemption under that Section of the 1933 Act, even if it does not comply with Regulation D.

Most companies do claim these exemptions under Regulation D, which consists of the following six rules:

1. Rule 501 contains definitions of various terms used in the Rules.

2. Rule 502 deals with general conditions and limitations and informational requirements applicable to some or all of the exemptions contained in Rules 504 through 506.

3. Rule 503 deals with SEC notification requirements.

4. Rule 504 provides an exemption for certain offerings of up to $1 million.

5. Rule 505 provides an exemption for certain offerings of up to $5 million in any 12-month period.

6. Rule 506 provides an exemption for certain offerings unlimited in amount.

Definitions

Rule 501 defines eight specific terms used in the Regulation. The most significant of these are discussed next.

Accredited Investors

Accredited investors are defined as those who are, or who the issuer reasonably believes are:

- Institutional investors, including banks;
- Savings and loan associations;
- Registered brokers and dealers;
- Insurance companies;
- Registered investment companies;
- Business development companies;
- Investment companies;
- Small business investment companies licensed by the SBA;
- Employee benefit plans subject to the Employee Retirement Income Security Act that have either a specified institutional fiduciary, total assets in excess of $5 million, or accredited persons making investment decisions;
- Employee benefit plans established by a state or an agency of the state, if such plan's total assets are greater than $5 million;
- Any corporation, business trust, partnership, or certain tax-exempt organizations with total assets in excess of $5 million (not formed to acquire the securities offered);
- Any director, executive officer, or general partner of the issuer;

- Any individual whose net worth, or joint net worth with spouse exceeds $1 million at the time of the purchase;
- Any individual who has had income in excess of $200,000 or joint income with spouse in excess of $300,000 in each of the last two years and who reasonably expects such income in the current year;
- Any trust with total assets in excess of $5 million (not formed to acquire the securities offered) directed by a sophisticated investor; and
- Any entity owned entirely by accredited investors.

Seek advice from your attorneys on what steps should be taken to support a "reasonable belief" that a prospective investor qualifies as an accredited investor.

Number of Purchasers

For the purposes of the specific exemptions in Rules 505 and 506, accredited investors and certain closely related parties need not be included in calculating the number of purchasers. In other words, an issuer may sell to an unlimited number of accredited investors in addition to the specified number of other purchasers. Also, certain corporations, partnerships, noncontributory employee benefit plans, and other entities may be counted as a single purchaser for this purpose.

General Conditions

The availability of Regulation D exemptions does not depend on the size of the company, and the exemptions under Rules 505 and 506 are available only to the issuer of securities and not to its affiliates or others for resale of the issuer's securities. The exemptions are also available for the issuance of securities in connection with a business combination.

The rules provide that certain offerings of the same securities may be considered as a single offering (i.e., "integrated"). Thus, they may be combined in determining whether the amount and numbers of purchasers comply with the exemptive provisions if those offerings are made within six months of the start or termination of the Regulation D offering.

Other general conditions for the use of Regulation D exemptions under Rules 505 and 506 are that there may be no general solicitation or general advertising in connection with the offering and that the issuer must follow certain procedures to ensure that the securities are not being acquired for public resale. These procedures include the exercise of reasonable care that a purchaser is not an underwriter or an agent for an underwriter, providing written disclosure of the resale limitations, and including a legend to that effect on the certificate itself.

Finally, any company relying on a Regulation D exemption must file a notice of sales of securities on a Form D. This notice must be filed with the SEC within 15 days of the first sale of securities. Companies must also be prepared to give the SEC, upon written request, copies of all information provided to purchasers of the securities. All such information would then become part of the public record.

Information Disclosure Requirements

The specific disclosure requirements under Regulation D vary according to whether the company is already an SEC registrant (i.e., a reporting company) and according to the size of the offering and the particular exemption claimed. All companies using a Rule 505 or Rule 506 exemption are subject to provisions dealing with the rights of nonaccredited investors to receive information furnished to accredited investors and the rights of all purchasers to ask questions of the issuer concerning the offering.

If the securities are sold only to accredited investors under any of the exemptions, or if the offering is $1 million or less, the SEC does not require any information to be furnished to investors. State laws and the investors themselves may nevertheless require certain information to be furnished.

Although the SEC does not impose informational disclosure requirements in some registration-exempt circumstances (such as those noted above), companies often issue an offering circular or memorandum. This decision, which should be made in consultation with your attorneys, depends on a variety of factors, including the number of offerees or purchasers, their existing relationship with the issuer, and their degree of investment sophistication. The SEC's antifraud provisions apply equally to registration-exempt offerings and lead many issuers to voluntarily make relevant disclosures as insurance against later charges by disgruntled investors that they were not informed of all material facts.

The information requirements for reporting companies are generally the same regardless of the size of the offering or the particular exemption claimed. The rules provide options as to information that must be provided, but it generally includes publicly available reports and filings, such as the most recent annual report to shareholders, Form 10-K, proxy statement, or registration statement.

Any other companies—including those going public for the first time, selling to one or more nonaccredited investors, and offering more than $1 million—are subject to specified information requirements.

OFFERINGS LIMITED TO $1 MILLION—RULE 504

This exemption is the least restrictive of the exemptions with respect to everything but the amount, which is limited to $1 million during a 12-month period. No restrictions are placed on the number or qualification of investors, and no information requirements are imposed. The exemption is directed at, and is well suited to, a small business seeking to raise a reasonably small amount of capital. It may not be used by investment companies, blank check companies, or reporting companies.

Unlike Rules 505 and 506, an exempt offering under Rule 504 allows general advertising and solicitation of investors. In addition, Rule 504 provides for free transferability (no resale restrictions) of securities acquired under Rule 504.

The $1 million offering price limitation is reduced by the amount of any sales of securities sold within the last 12 months in violation of the registration provisions of the 1933 Act or exempt from registration by this Rule, Rule 505, or Regulation A (discussed next).

OFFERINGS LIMITED TO $5 MILLION—RULE 505

This exemption increases the amount that may be offered and also imposes some additional restrictions. The exemption is available to all issuers except investment companies and issuers disqualified because of specified acts of misconduct with respect to the securities laws. These so-called "bad boy" provisions apply not only to the issuer and its officers, directors, general partners, and major shareholders, but also to the underwriters and their partners, directors, and officers. Whether or not the issuer is aware of a prior disqualifying act of misconduct by one of the aforementioned, the exemption would be unavailable. Therefore, you must exercise extreme care and consult your attorneys to guard against such an event.

The exemption also limits the number of purchasers to 35 nonaccredited investors. However, no limit is placed on the number of accredited investors. Certain related persons may be excluded and certain other entities may be counted as one purchaser in calculating the number of purchasers (see "Number of Purchasers").

Unless the securities are sold exclusively to accredited investors, certain information requirements are specified, as discussed earlier (see "Information Disclosure Requirements").

And, as with the Rule 504 exemption, the $5 million offering price limitation for this exemption is reduced by the amount of any sales of securities sold within the last 12 months in violation of the registration provisions of the 1933 Act or exempt from registration by this Rule, Rule 504, or Regulation A (discussed next).

UNLIMITED PRIVATE PLACEMENTS—RULE 506

This registration exemption is available to any issuer, including investment companies and reporting companies, and is not subject to "bad boy" provisions. It may be used for offerings of any amount.

The number of purchasers is limited to 35 nonaccredited investors, but no limit is placed on the number of accredited investors. However, certain "sophistication" requirements are imposed for nonaccredited investors (in contrast to Rules 504 and 505). Specifically, the issuer must reasonably believe that each nonaccredited investor, either alone or with his purchaser representative, has enough knowledge and experience in financial and business matters to be able to evaluate the merits and risks of the prospective investment. The provision on sophistication relates to purchasers, not necessarily to offerees. Accredited investors are presumed to be sophisticated.

Unless the securities are sold exclusively to accredited investors, certain information requirements are specified, as discussed earlier (see "Information Disclosure Requirements").

ACCREDITED INVESTOR OFFERINGS UP TO $5 MILLION—SECTION 4(6)

Section 4(6), created in 1980, exempts from registration any offers and sales of up to $5 million by an issuer if they are made exclusively to accredited investors. This exemption is similar to the Regulation D, Rule 505 limited offering exemption, and compliance with Rule 505 normally would constitute compliance with Section 4(6).

However, some important differences might make a Section 4(6) accredited investor offering available to an issuer not able to use a Rule 505 limited offering exemption. Specifically, Section 4(6) does not contain the "bad boy" provisions that may block some issuers' use of Rule 505. And Section 4(6) is available to investment companies, while Rule 505 is not. Additionally, subject to the general integration rules discussed earlier, the $5 million limit on Section 4(6) offerings is not reduced by sales in the previous 12 months under Rules 504 or 505, Regulation A.

Apart from these differences, the provisions of Section 4(6) are similar to those of Rule 505 with respect to accredited investor offerings. The definition of "accredited investors" is the same, no advertising or general solicitation is allowed, no information requirements are mandated, and similar SEC notification requirements are imposed.

COORDINATION WITH STATE EXEMPTIONS

After Regulation D was adopted by the SEC, the North American Securities Administrators' Association (NASAA) developed a Uniform Limited Offering Exemption (ULOE) that has been adopted by numerous states with some variations. Your attorneys will advise you on the availability of these state exemptions.

However, while the recently adopted small business initiatives reduced the regulatory burden placed on small businesses by federal agencies, the SEC's effort was not coordinated with the various state securities regulators. Accordingly, certain advantages provided by the small business initiatives are subject to overriding restrictions placed on the company by the state securities' regulations. For example, the ability to "test the waters" under Regulation A requires similar state action to provide the proclaimed benefits and potential cost savings. Many states currently prohibit companies from soliciting potential interest in a proposed offering prior to the filing of a registration statement with the SEC.

The SEC has continued the theme of reduced regulatory burden for small business issuers. This is evidenced by the reduced reporting requirements in annual meeting proxy statements for small businesses that were adopted in October 1992. The SEC has acknowledged that the small business initiatives have not received the anticipated support from the state regulators.

Accordingly, the SEC may take a step backward and revisit the small business initiatives in cooperation with the state securities regulators before proceeding with additional small business initiatives.

INTRASTATE OFFERINGS—RULE 147

The 1933 Act exempts from registration any security that is offered and sold only to residents of a single state by an issuer that is resident and doing business in such state. Through the years, judicial and administrative interpretations of this section have resulted in various ambiguities and also some abuses of this exemption.

The exemption is available to all issuers, regardless of size, and without limitations on the amount of the offering or the number or financial sophistication of purchasers. However, restrictions are imposed to ensure that the exemption is used only for genuinely local offerings. In response to the problems this created for both issuers and the SEC, the SEC in 1974 adopted Rule 147. This rule provides more objective, but also more restrictive, criteria for determining compliance with the exemption.

The SEC notes that "the exemption was intended to apply only to issues genuinely local in character, which in reality represent local financing by the local industries, carried out through local investment." Accordingly, Rule 147 provides objective standards for determining whether an issuer is resident in and doing business within the state, and whether offerees and purchasers are resident in the state.

An issuer is considered resident in a state if it is incorporated or organized in that state or, in the case of general partnerships and other such organizations not organized under any state law, if the principal office is located in that state.

An issuer is deemed to be doing business in a state if it derives at least 80 percent of its consolidated gross revenue from that state, has at least 80 percent of its consolidated assets in the state, intends to use (and does use) 80 percent of the net proceeds of the offering in the state, and has its principal office in the state.

A company or other business organization must have its principal office in a state, and individuals must have their principal residence in a state, to be deemed to be a resident of that state. Note that these residence requirements apply not only to purchasers, but also to offerees.

To ensure that the securities "come to rest in the hands of resident investors," the rule also imposes a limitation on resale of the securities. For nine months after the issuer's last sale of the securities, any resale may be made only to other residents of the state. As a precaution against sales and resales made to out-of-state investors, the issuer is required to disclose in writing the limitations on resale and must obtain written representation from each purchaser as to residence. In addition, a legend must be printed on the securities stating that the securities have not been registered and noting the resale limitations.

One of the primary drawbacks of this exemption is the potential exposure to the issuer if even one share is sold, either initially or resold within nine months, to a nonresident of the state. This risk can be substantial, particularly if the offering is anticipated to be widely distributed. Although various precautions are prescribed, and other precautions can be taken, the rules of this exemption are absolute: A disqualifying sale can subject the entire offering to potential rescission, regardless of any precautions taken by the issuer.

Rule 147 does not prescribe any informational disclosures. However, the offering is not exempt from the antifraud provisions or applicable state securities laws.

UNREGISTERED PUBLIC OFFERINGS UP TO $5 MILLION—REGULATION A

Regulation A provides an exemption from registration for certain offerings of up to $5 million in a 12-month period. The exemption is available to U.S. and Canadian issuers except existing registrants, investment companies, blank check companies, and issuers of individual interest in certain of oil, gas, or other mineral rights. And the regulation's "bad boy" provisions (similar to those discussed earlier under Rule 505 of Regulation D) preclude use of the exemption if the issuer, its underwriters, or any of its directors, officers, or principals have engaged in certain specified acts of misconduct.

Regulation A imposes no restrictions on the number or qualification of investors or on resale of the securities, if the issuer has had net income from continuing operations in at least one of its last two fiscal years. It also permits certain advertising and general solicitation generally referred to as "testing the waters" as discussed in Chapter 8. Thus, in many respects it is similar to going public with a registered public offering. But, as with the other registration exemptions, use of the Regulation A exemption does not in itself trigger the 1934 Act's periodic reporting obligations.

Regulation A requires that an offering circular be provided to investors at least 48 hours prior to mailing a confirmation of sale. Issuers can choose to provide, in the offering statement, narrative disclosure required by Part I of Form SB-2, or the traditional registration disclosure format. Corporate issuers have the option of using a question-and-answer format (the "SCOR form") used in many states, in addition to the aforementioned choices. The circular is similar to a prospectus, and must be filed as part of the offering statement (Form 1-A), which is reviewed and cleared by the SEC.

Two years of financial statements must be included, although no audit requirements are imposed. However, many underwriters and state laws may nevertheless require audited financial statements. If audited financial statements are otherwise required, they are included in the offering circular.

COMPARISON OF REGISTRATION FORMS S-1 AND SB-2

	Form S-1	Form SB-2
Purpose	Registration of securities with the SEC under the 1933 Act	Registration of securities with the SEC under the 1993 Act
Dollar • Registrant • Secondary offering	No limit No limit	No limit No limit
Eligibility for use	No restrictions	Companies must meet the definition of a small-business issuer as defined in Item 10 of Regulation S-B
Significant required disclosures	Summary information, risk factors, and ratio of earnings to fixed charges (S-K Item 503)	Same as S-1, except the ratio of earnings to fixed charges need not be presented (S-B Item 503)
	Use of proceeds; determination of offering price; dilution; selling security holders; plan of distribution; description of securities to be registered; interests of named experts and counsel (S-K Items 504–509 and Item 202)	Same as S-1 (S-B Items 504–509 and Item 202)
	Description of the business (S-K Item 101)	Less extensive than S-1 (S-B Item 101)
	Description of property (S-K Item 102)	Less extensive than S-1 (S-B Item 102)
	Legal proceedings (S-K Item 103)	Same as S-1 (S-B Item 103)
	Market and dividend data (S-K Item 201)	Less extensive than S-1 (S-B Item 201)
	Financial statements must comply with Regulation S-X and	Financial statements prepared in accordance with generally

	Form S-1	Form SB-2
Significant required disclosures (*continued*)	generally accepted accounting principles; additional financial statements are required for investees[a] and for significant acquired or to-be acquired companies[b]	accepted accounting principles; additional financial statements are required for significant acquired or to-be-acquired companies[c]
	• Two years' audited balance sheets, updated by a condensed interim balance sheet as required	One year's audited balance sheet, updated by a condensed interim balance sheet as required
	• Three years' audited statements of income and cash flows, and reconciliations of other shareholders' equity accounts, updated by comparative condensed interim statements as required	Two years' audited statements of income and cash flows, and reconciliations of other shareholders' equity accounts, updated by comparative condensed interim statements as required
	• Financial statements and schedules required by S-X	No schedules
	Selected financial data; supplementary financial information; management's discussion and analysis of financial condition and result of operations; and disagreements with auditors on financial and disclosure matters (S-K Items 301–304)	Selected financial data and supplemental financial information not required; management's discussion and analysis of financial condition and results of operations less extensive than S-1; and disagreements with auditors on financial and disclosure matters same as S-1 (S-B Items 303 and 304)

	Form S-1	Form SB-2
Significant required disclosures (*continued*)	Information about directors and executive officers (S-K Item 401)	Same as S-1 (S-B Item 401)
	Executive compensation and transactions with management (S-K Items 402 and 404)	Less extensive than S-1 (S-B Items 402 and 404)
	Ownership of securities by certain beneficial owners and management (S-K Item 403)	Same as S-1 (S-B Item 403)

[a] Financial statements need not be audited for those years in which the significance test in rule 3-09 of Regulation S-X is not met; interim financial statements are required in a Form S-1.

[b] The number of years for which financial statements are required is determined by the significance test in rule 3-05 of Regulation S-X; interim financial statements are required.

[c] The number of years for which financial statements are required is determined by the significance tests in Item 310(3) of Regulation S-B; interim financial statements are required.

OUTLINE FOR A BUSINESS PLAN

The following is an outline of suggested topics for inclusion in a business plan and certain other suggestions on writing an effective business plan:

I. Executive Summary

The Executive Summary should not be a mere listing of topics contained in the body of your business plan but should emphasize the key issues presented. A critical point that must be communicated in the Executive Summary is your company's distinctive competence—the factors that will make your business successful in a competitive market.

A. The Purpose of the Plan

1. Attract investors

2. Document an operational plan for controlling the business

B. Market Analysis

1. The characteristics of your target market (demographic, geographic, etc.)

2. The size of your target market

C. The Company

1. The needs your company will satisfy
2. The products or services you will offer to satisfy those needs

D. Marketing and Sales Activities

1. Marketing strategy
2. Sales strategy
3. Keys to success in your competitive environment

E. Product or Service Research and Development

1. Major milestones
2. Ongoing efforts

F. Organization and Personnel

1. Key managers and owners
2. Key operations employees

G. Financial Data

1. Funds required and their use
2. Historical financial summary
3. Prospective financial summary (including a brief justification for prospective sales levels)

If your company is new, you could be sending your business plan to potential investors who review hundreds of them each year. More often than not, these individuals do not get past the Executive Summary of the plans they receive. Your Executive Summary must therefore give the reader a useful understanding of your business and make the point of most interest to them, "What is in it for the investor?"

In total, your Executive Summary should be less than three pages in length and provide the reader with a succinct overview of your entire business plan.

The Executive Summary should be followed by a brief Table of Contents designed to assist readers in locating specific sections in the plan. Detailed descriptions of the plan's contents should be avoided in the Table of Contents.

II. Market Analysis

The Market Analysis section should reflect your knowledge of your industry and present highlights and analysis of your market research. Detailed market research studies, however, should be presented as appendices to your plan.

A. Industry Description and Outlook

1. Description of your primary industry
2. Size of the industry
   a. Historically
   b. Currently
   c. In five years
   d. In ten years
3. Industry characteristics and trends (Where is it in its life cycle?)
   a. Historically
   b. Currently
   c. In the future
4. Major customer groups
   a. Businesses
   b. Governments
   c. Consumers

B. Target Markets

1. Distinguishing characteristics of your primary target markets and market segments. Narrow your target markets to a manageable size. Efforts to penetrate target markets that are too broad are often ineffective.
   a. Critical needs
   b. Extent to which those needs are currently being met
   c. Demographics
   d. Geographic location

    e. Purchase decision makers and influencers

    f. Seasonal/cyclical trends

2. Primary target market size

    a. Number of prospective customers

    b. Annual purchases of products or services meeting the same or similar needs as your products or services

    c. Geographic area

    d. Anticipated market growth

3. Market penetration—indicates the extent to which you anticipate penetrating your market and demonstrates why you feel that level of penetration is achievable based on your market research.

    a. Market share

    b. Number of customers

    c. Geographic coverage

    d. Rationale for market penetration estimates

4. Pricing/gross margin targets

    a. Price levels

    b. Gross margin levels

    c. Discount structure (volume, prompt payment, etc.)

5. Methods by which specific members of your target market can be identified

    a. Directories

    b. Trade association publications

    c. Government documents

6. Media through which you can communicate with specific members of your target market

    a. Publications

    b. Radio/television broadcasts

    c. Sources of influence/advice

7. Purchasing cycle of potential customers
   a. Need identification
   b. Research for solutions to needs
   c. Solution evaluation process
   d. Final solution selection responsibility and authority (executives, purchasing agents, engineers, etc.)
8. Key trends and anticipated changes within your primary target markets
9. Secondary target markets and key attributes
   a. Needs
   b. Demographics
   c. Significant future trends

C. Market Test Results

1. Potential customers contacted
2. Information/demonstrations given to potential customers
3. Reaction of potential customers
4. Importance of satisfaction of targeted needs
5. Test group's willingness to purchase products/services at various price levels

D. Lead Times (amount of time between customer order placement and product/service delivery)

1. Initial orders
2. Reorders
3. Volume purchases

E. Competition

1. Identification (by product line or service and market segment)
   a. Existing
   b. Market share

c. Potential (How long will your "window of opportunity" be open before your initial success breeds new competition? Who will your new competitors likely be?)

d. Direct

e. Indirect

2. Strengths (competitive advantages)

a. Ability to satisfy customer needs

b. Market penetration

c. Track record and reputation

d. Staying power (financial resources)

e. Key personnel

3. Weaknesses (competitive disadvantages)

a. Ability to satisfy customer needs

b. Market penetration

c. Track record and reputation

d. Staying power (financial resources)

e. Key personnel

4. Importance of your target market to your competition

5. Barriers to entry into the market

a. Cost (investment)

b. Time

c. Technology

d. Key personnel

e. Customer inertia (brand loyalty, existing relationships, etc.)

f. Existing patents and trademarks

F. Regulatory Restrictions

1. Customer or governmental regulatory requirements

    a. Methods for meeting the requirements

    b. Timing involved

    c. Cost

  2. Anticipated changes in regulatory requirements

Since your market analysis provides the only basis for your prospective sales and pricing estimates, make sure that this section clearly demonstrates that there is a market need for your product or service, that you as owner not only understand this need but can meet it, and that you can sell at a profit. This section should also include an estimate of your market penetration annually for the next five years.

III. Company Description

The Company Description section must provide an overview of how all of the elements of your company fit together without going into detail, since most of the subjects will be covered in depth elsewhere in the plan.

A. Nature of Your Business

  1. Marketplace needs to be satisfied

  2. Method(s) of need satisfaction (products and services)

  3. Individuals/organizations with the needs

B. Your Distinctive Competences (primary factors that will lead to your success)

  1. Superior customer need satisfaction

  2. Production/service delivery efficiencies

  3. Personnel

  4. Geographic location

Writing this section is the first real test of your ability to communicate the essence of your business. Since the lack of a clear description of the key concepts of your company will indicate to the reader that you have not yet clearly defined it in your own mind, you must be certain that this section concisely and accurately describes the substance of your new business.

IV. Marketing and Sales Activities

Both general and specific information must be included in this part of your plan. Your objective is to describe the activities that will allow you to meet the sales and margin levels indicated in your prospective financial statements.

A. Overall Marketing Strategy

1. Marketing penetration strategy
2. Growth strategy
   a. Internal
   b. Acquisition
   c. Franchise
   d. Horizontal (providing similar products to different users)
   e. Vertical (providing the products at different levels of the distribution chain)
3. Distribution channels (include discount/profitability levels at each stage)
   a. Original equipment manufacturers
   b. Internal sales force
   c. Distributors
   d. Retailers
4. Communication
   a. Promotion
   b. Advertising
   c. Public relations
   d. Personal selling
   e. Printed materials (catalogues, brochures, etc.)

B. Sales Strategies

1. Sales force

   a. Internal vs. independent representatives (advantages and disadvantages of your strategy)

   b. Size

   c. Recruitment and training

   d. Compensation

2. Sales activities

   a. Identifying prospects

   b. Prioritizing prospects

   c. Number of sales calls made per period

   d. Average number of sales calls per sale

   e. Average dollar size per sale

   f. Average dollar size per reorder

Do not underestimate the importance of presenting a well-conceived sales strategy here. Without an efficient approach to beating a path to the doors of potential customers, companies with very good products and services often fail.

V. Products and Services

Special attention should be paid to the users of your business plan as you develop this section. Too much detail will have a negative impact on most external users of the plan. Avoid turning this section of your business plan into a policies and procedures manual for your employees.

A. Detailed Product/Service Description (from the user's perspective)

1. Specific benefits of product/service

2. Ability to meet needs

3. Competitive advantages

4. Present state (idea, prototype, small production runs, etc.)

B. Product Life Cycle

1. Description of the product/service's current position within its life cycle
2. Factors that might change the anticipated life cycle
   a. Lengthen it
   b. Shorten it

C. Copyrights, Patents, and Trade Secrets

1. Existing or pending copyrights or patents
2. Anticipated copyright and patent filings
3. Key aspects of your products or services that cannot be patented or copyrighted
4. Key aspects of your products or services that qualify as trade secrets
5. Existing legal agreements with owners and employees
   a. Nondisclosure agreements
   b. Noncomplete agreements

D. Research and Development Activities

1. Activities in process
2. Future activities (include milestones)
3. Anticipated results of future research and development activities
   a. New products or services
   b. New generations of existing products or services
   c. Complementary products or services
   d. Replacement products or services
4. Research and development activities of others in your industry
   a. Direct competitors
   b. Indirect competitors

c. Suppliers

d. Customers

The emphasis in this section should be on your company's unique ability to satisfy the needs of the marketplace. Avoid criticizing your competition's products too severely in this section because the natural tendency of a reader who is not part of your organization will be to empathize with the unrepresented party—your competition. Concentrate on the positive aspects of your product's ability to meet existing market needs and allow your readers to come to their own conclusions about your competition based on the objective information presented here and in the Market Analysis section.

VI. Operations

Here again, too much detail can detract from the rest of your plan. Be certain that the level of detail included fits the specific needs of the plan's users.

A. Production and Service Delivery Procedures

1. Internal
2. External (subcontractors)

B. Production and Service Delivery Capability

1. Internal
2. External (subcontractors)
3. Anticipated increases in capacity

    a. Investment

    b. New cost factors (direct and indirect)

    c. Timing

C. Operating Competitive Advantages

1. Techniques
2. Experience
3. Economies of scale
4. Lower direct costs

D. Suppliers

1. Identification of the suppliers of critical elements of production
   a. Primary
   b. Secondary
2. Lead time requirements
3. Evaluation of the risks of critical element shortages
4. Description of the existing and anticipated contractual relationships with suppliers

Since many of the aspects of your new business are still theoretical at this point, special care must be taken to be sure the specifics of your operations do not conflict with the information included in your prospective financial statements. Any inconsistencies between those two areas will result in some unpleasant surprises as your company begins operations.

VII. Management and Ownership

Your management team's talents and skills are some of the few truly unique aspects of your company. If you are going to use your plan to attract investors, this section must emphasize your management's talents and skills, and indicate why they are a part of your company's distinctive competence that cannot easily be replicated by your competition. Remember that individuals invest in people, not ideas.

Do not use this section of the plan to negotiate future ownership of the company with potential investors. Simply explain the current ownership.

A. Management Staff Structure

1. Management staff organization chart
2. Narrative description of the chart

B. Key Managers (complete resumes should be presented in an appendix to the business plan)

1. Name
2. Position

3. Brief position description, including primary duties

4. Primary responsibilities and authority with previous employers

5. Unique skills and experiences that add to your company's distinctive competences

6. Compensation basis and levels (be sure they are reasonable—not too high and not too low)

C. Planned Additions to the Current Management Team

1. Position

2. Primary responsibilities and authority

3. Requisite skills and experience

4. Recruitment process

5. Timing of employment

6. Anticipated contribution to the company's success

7. Compensation basis and levels (be sure they are in line with the market)

D. Legal Structure of the Business

1. Corporation

    a. C corporation

    b. S corporation

2. Partnership

    a. General

    b. Limited

3. Proprietorship

E. Owners

1. Names

2. Percentage ownership

3. Extent of involvement with the company

    4. Form of ownership

        a. Common stock

        b. Preferred stock

        c. General partner

        d. Limited partner

    5. Outstanding equity equivalents

        a. Options

        b. Warrants

        c. Convertible debt

    6. Common stock

        a. Authorized

        b. Issued

F. Board of Directors

    1. Names

    2. Position on the board

    3. Extent of involvement with the company

    4. Background

    5. Contribution to the company's success

        a. Historically

        b. In the future

Since your management team *is* unique, make sure that you stress their backgrounds and skills and how they will contribute to the success of your product/service and business. This is especially important to emphasize when you are looking for financing.

VIII. Funds Required and Their Uses

Any new or additional funding reflected in your prospective financial statements should be discussed here. Alternative funding scenarios can be presented if appropriate, and corresponding prospective financial statements are presented in subsequent sections of your plan.

A. Current Funding Requirements

1. Amount
2. Timing
3. Type
   a. Equity
   b. Debt
   c. Mezzanine
4. Terms

B. Funding Requirements over the Next Five Years

1. Amount
2. Timing
3. Type
   a. Equity
   b. Debt
   c. Mezzanine
4. Terms

C. Use of Funds

1. Capital expenditures
2. Working capital
3. Debt retirement
4. Acquisitions

D. Long-Range Financial Strategies (liquidating investors' positions)

1. Going public
2. Leveraged buyout
3. Acquisition by another company
4. Debt service levels and timing
5. Liquidation of the venture

Remember that since the rate of return is their most important consideration—and that the initial public offering market is sometimes not available—investors will be looking for alternative exit strategies. Therefore, be flexible and creative in developing these opportunities, taking into consideration such recent trends as a merger/acquisition and strategic partnering. Although details can be worked out later, investors need to know that you understand their primary objectives as you develop your overall business strategy.

IX. Financial Data

The Financial Data section contains the financial representation of all the information presented in the other sections. Various prospective scenarios can be included, if appropriate.

A. Historical Financial Data (past three to five years, if applicable)
   1. Annual statements
      a. Income
      b. Balance sheet
      c. Cash flows
   2. Name of CPA firm and type of report
      a. Audit
      b. Review
      c. Compilation

B. Prospective Financial Data (next five years)
   1. Next year (by month or quarter)
      a. Income
      b. Balance sheet
      c. Cash flows
      d. Capital expenditure budget
   2. Final four years (by quarter and/or year)
      a. Income
      b. Balance sheet
      c. Cash flows
      d. Capital expenditure budget

   3. Summary of significant assumptions
   4. Type of prospective financial data
      a. Forecast (management's best estimate)
      b. Projection ("what-if" scenarios)
   5. Level of CPA involvement
      a. Assembly
      b. Agreed-upon procedures
      c. Review
      d. Examination

C. Analysis

   1. Historical financial statements
      a. Ratio analysis
      b. Trend analysis with graphic presentation
   2. Prospective financial statements
      a. Ratio analysis
      b. Trend analysis with graphic presentation

The Financial Data section of your business plan is another area where specialized knowledge can be invaluable. If you do not have someone with sufficient financial expertise on your management team, you will probably need to utilize an outside advisor.

X. Appendices or Exhibits

Any additional detailed or confidential information that could be useful to the readers of the business plan but was not appropriate for distribution to everyone receiving the body of the plan can be presented here. Accordingly, appendices and exhibits should be bound separately from the other sections of the plan and provided on an as-needed basis to readers.

A. Resumes of Key Managers

B. Pictures of Products

C. Professional References

D. Market Studies

E. Pertinent Published Information

    1. Magazine articles

    2. References to books

F. Patents

G. Significant Contracts

    1. Leases

    2. Sales contracts

    3. Purchases contracts

    4. Partnership/ownership agreements

    5. Stock option agreements

    6. Employment/compensation agreements

    7. Noncompete agreements

    8. Insurance

        a. Product liability

        b. Officers' and directors' liability

        c. General liability

In some instances, the thicker the business plan, the less likely a potential investor is to read it thoroughly. However, you do want to be able to demonstrate to potential funding sources that you have done a complete job in preparing your plan and that the comments made within it are well documented. By properly utilizing appendices and exhibits, you can make the size of your business plan palatable to its users and still have the additional information they may require readily available.

APPENDIX G

COMPENSATION STRATEGIES

As a public company, you will be making compensation decisions in a more public environment. You will need to communicate your pay policies not only to employees, but also to regulators, stock exchange officials, investors, and the public at large.

Further, as a public company, you have a powerful new element for your company's compensation plans: publicly traded equity—both in the form of outright stock grants and in the form of options.

For these reasons, you will need to reevaluate your company's basic compensation goals. Do you need to make special efforts to attract, retain, and motivate star talent at the top, or is now the time to take an organization-wide look at incentive compensation? Are your managers and employees truly willing to accept more performance-based "risk" in their compensation, or is security still a dominant need? Should your compensation strategy focus on long-term incentives, or do you need to weigh your compensation plans toward short-term performance rewards?

These questions are offered as an aid when reviewing your compensation strategies. Now is the time to "think big," asking yourself why you will be paying people and why they will be working for you.

In order to convert your compensation strategy into a viable plan, it will be helpful to ask questions about who will get compensation, in what form, for what purpose, and when.

PAY RECIPIENTS: MANAGERS/EMPLOYEES/DIRECTORS

You should consider entering into employment agreements with your most valuable employees and disclose the existence of those agreements in your prospectus—not only because it is required to be disclosed in your registration statement, but also to assure underwriters and investors that you have done what you can to prevent departures in the near term that could harm the company.

PAY FORM: CASH/STOCK

What amount of stock vs. cash do you wish to use for compensation? What about benefits? Granting your key managers a meaningful amount of equity provides a valuable tool to motivate them—and to impress investors. By linking management performance to company performance, you can improve both.

Underwriters and analysts like to see a strong element of risk in compensation plans. A clearly communicated policy that includes risk—especially through stock awards—can lead to positive underwriter and analyst assessments. This in turn can lead to higher stock prices and increased "pay power" for stock-based plans.

As you set the stock ownership level for each employee, try to find a level and timing of ownership that will motivate the employee to make decisions, not avoid them. You want to energize, not entrench. If ownership is too high, and too closely tied to short-term stock price gains, this can cause an employee to become risk-averse.

In addition to actual awards, you may wish to set targets for employee stock ownership. To achieve the target levels, you can grant stock, stock options, and/or warrants—or set voluntary or mandatory minimums for employee stock purchases.

Stock awards are not the only way to build more risk into compensation. Another way to do this is to move from fixed to variable cash pay based on specific performance measures. Risk-based pay sends a strong message to the market, and will go a long way toward helping the underwriter market your stock at a premium price.

PURPOSE: PAST/FUTURE

How have you balanced rewards for past performance vs. incentives for future performance? How would you like to modify this mix as you go public?

If rapid growth or other factors have prevented you from making rewards commensurate with achievement, you may wish to build rewards into your plan from the beginning. This can help you retain managers now.

If, on the other hand, you have already rewarded your management team and employees generously for past performance, you may wish to structure a more forward-looking compensation program that emphasizes incentives over rewards.

An increasing number of companies are granting performance-based stock options keyed to earnings per share (EPS), stock price, or the meeting of strategic targets, adjusting targets from year to year. This kind of device can help you retain managers down the road.

Your plan also could have elements of both past and future reward. In that regard, many companies will grant a large number of stock options immediately prior to the IPO coupled with a plan to grant additional options over time.

Whether your rewards are for past or future performance, it is important to articulate it in your offering documents from the beginning. Nobody likes surprises.

PAY TIMING: NOW/LATER

When will you award pay? Do you want to grant all available stock now, or reserve some for a later time? If you grant all the available stock now and need some later, will you buy back stock, issue more, or depend exclusively on options?

Again, there are trade-offs. If previous compensation levels were relatively low, you may want to grant stock generously at all appropriate levels fairly quickly. On the other hand, if you use up all your grantable stock going into the IPO, you may motivate managers and employees and thrill Wall Street in the short-term, but you could narrow your choices for the long haul.

Therefore, you may wish to make moderate stock awards now, reserving some stock for later, over a two- to five-year period. Or you may wish to put the burden on the employee to purchase the stock by announcing target goals—or requirements—for share purchase.

In any case, option plans that phase in over time are always a good idea. Even if you are rewarding your employees generously going into the IPO, you will need to find ways to provide additional rewards and incentives later on.

All of these decisions can have significant accounting and tax consequences, so you should consult with your professional advisors during the process of formulating your compensation plan.

Begin by setting your basic compensation goals. Then move toward achieving those goals by giving the right rewards to the right people for the right reasons at the right time. And finally, be sure to disclose your significant compensation plans in your prospectus.

GLOSSARY

ACCREDITED INVESTORS—Individual or institutional investors who meet the qualifying SEC criteria with respect to financial sophistication or financial assets.

AFTER MARKET—Trading in an issuer's securities once the company has gone public. After market trading is between third parties and does not involve the issuer.

ALL-HANDS MEETING—A meeting of all the parties involved in preparing the registration statement, including company management, the company's attorneys, auditors, underwriters, and the underwriters' attorneys.

ANALYST—A specialist, often employed by an investment banking firm, who follows certain companies and analyzes their financial statements for the purpose of providing investment advice.

BAD BOY PROVISIONS—Provisions that disqualify issuers from using certain registration exemptions if certain individuals involved in the offering have engaged in specified acts of misconduct with respect to the securities laws.

BECOMING EFFECTIVE—The date and time the SEC declares the IPO offering effective and sales of stock can begin.

BEST EFFORTS UNDERWRITING—A type of underwriting agreement in which the underwriters only agree to use their best efforts to sell the shares on the issuer's behalf. The underwriters do not commit to purchase any unsold shares. (See, in contrast, **FIRM COMMITMENT UNDERWRITING**.)

BLANK CHECK COMPANY—A company that raises capital to invest in a business opportunity that has not been identified at the time of the offering.

Blue Sky Laws—A common term for state securities laws. Blue sky laws are not uniform across the states and must be complied with in any state in which shares will be offered, not just sold.

Blue Sky Memorandum—A memorandum, usually prepared by the underwriters' attorneys, which sets forth the various securities law provisions and restrictions applicable to each of the states in which the offering may be made.

Bridge Financing—Financing obtained by a company expecting to secure permanent financing (e.g., through an initial public offering) within a short time, such as two years.

Bring Down Letter—The update to the **Comfort Letter** issued as a condition of closing an IPO offering. The bring down letter reaffirms the detailed comfort issued when the offering becomes effective.

Capitalization—The company's debt and equity structure.

Cheap Stock—Common stock issued to selected persons (e.g., company insiders and promoters) within one year of a public offering at a price less than the public offering price. (Also applies to stock options, warrants, or other potentially dilutive instruments.)

Closing Meeting—The final meeting for the purpose of exchanging company securities for the proceeds of the offering. The closing meeting generally will occur five business days after the commencement of the offering to allow the underwriter sufficient time to collect the proceeds from its customers.

Comfort Letter—A letter provided by a company's independent auditors detailing procedures performed at the request of the underwriters. The letter supplements the underwriters' due diligence review.

Comment Letter—A letter from the staff of the SEC describing deficiencies noted in its review of a registration statement. Comment letters request additional information or that changes be made before the offering can become effective and the shares offered to investors.

CONSENT—In a securities offering, usually refers to the company's auditors giving their consent for the use of their audit report on prior year's financial statements in a registration statement. Such financial statements cannot be used in a registration statement without the accountant's consent. Thus, the CPAs will update their work to confirm the continuing validity of their audit report.

DILUTION—The effect on prospective purchasers' equity interest caused by a disparity between the public offering price per share and the tangible book value per share immediately preceding the offering.

DUE DILIGENCE—The responsibility of those preparing and signing the registration statement to conduct an investigation in order to provide a reasonable basis for their belief that statements made in the registration statement are true and do not omit any material facts.

EFFECTIVE DATE—The date on which the registration statement becomes effective and actual sales of the securities can begin.

EMPLOYEE STOCK OWNERSHIP PLAN (ESOP)—A tax-favored type of employee benefit plan providing a vehicle for employee ownership of a company.

EXEMPT OFFERING—An offering exempt from most of the detailed and time-consuming SEC registration requirements.

FINANCIAL ACCOUNTING STANDARDS BOARD—The primary private-sector body responsible for establishing accounting standards.

FINANCIAL REPORTING RELEASES (FRR)—Releases from the SEC announcing new or revised rules (e.g., amendments to Regulation S-X or S-K and to the various forms) and matters of general accounting and auditing interest.

FIRM COMMITMENT UNDERWRITING—A type of underwriting agreement in which the underwriters agree to purchase all the shares in the offering and then resell them to the public. Any shares not sold to the public are paid for and held by the underwriters for their own account.

FOREIGN CORRUPT PRACTICES ACT (FCPA)—Enacted in 1977, the FCPA requires all public companies to maintain adequate accounting records and an adequate system of internal controls, and prohibits certain payments from being made to specified foreign officials and politicians.

FORM 8-A—An abbreviated form for registration of a class of securities under the 1934 Act.

FORM 8-K—A report required to be filed with the SEC when certain material events have occurred.

FORM 10-K—The annual report required to be filed with the SEC.

FORM 10-KSB—The annual report to be filed with the SEC by small business issuers electing to file under Regulation S-B.

FORM 10-Q—The quarterly report required to be filed with the SEC.

FORM 10-QSB—The quarterly report required to be filed with the SEC by small business issuers electing to file under Regulation S-B.

FORM S-1—The most comprehensive registration statement, used by issuers who are not eligible to use any of the abbreviated registration forms or the forms available to small business issuers.

FORM S-2—A registration statement used by certain seasoned companies that permits incorporation by reference of the annual report (and other periodic reports, as applicable) and requires delivery of the latest annual report to investors.

FORM S-3—A registration statement used by certain seasoned companies, which also permits incorporation by reference of the annual report (and other periodic reports as applicable), but does not require delivery of the latest annual report to investors.

FORM S-4—An abbreviated registration statement typically used to register securities to be issued in connection with Rule 145 transactions involving certain reclassifications, mergers, consolidations and transfers of assets; exchange offers for securities of the issuer or another entity; and reoffers or resales of securities registered on the form.

FORM SB-1—A short-form registration statement that may be utilized by small business issuers for both initial and repeat offerings, and for both primary and secondary offerings. May be used to register securities offerings of up to $10 million in any continuous 12-month period, excluding securities registered on Form S-8.

FORM SB-2—A short-form registration statement that may be utilized by small business issuers for both initial and repeat offerings, and for both primary and secondary offerings.

FORM SR—A report required to be filed periodically with the SEC, during and after an offering, describing the amount of proceeds from the offering to date and the use of the proceeds.

GENERALLY ACCEPTED ACCOUNTING PRINCIPLE (GAAP)—Accounting practices established by recognized standard setting bodies or through practice.

GREEN SHOE OPTION—An overallotment option granted to underwriters that allows them to purchase up to a specified number of additional shares from the company in the event that they sell more shares than allocated to them in the underwriting agreement. The Green Shoe Corporation was the first company to use the technique.

INSIDER TRADING—Trading in a company's securities by company insiders or others with access to nonpublic information about the company.

INTRASTATE OFFERINGS—An SEC-registration exempt offering made only to residents of the state in which the issuer resides and carries on its business.

INVESTMENT BANKERS—Specialists who advise companies on available sources of financing, advise on the optimal time for a public offering of securities, and often also act as underwriters for a public offering.

LEAD UNDERWRITER—The underwriter that manages a securities offering. Traditionally, the lead underwriter is listed on the left on the cover of a prospectus. Also called managing underwriter. The lead underwriter acts on behalf of the underwriting syndicate.

LETTER OF INTENT—A preliminary agreement between the underwriters and a company specifying the terms that will be contained in the actual underwriting agreement. This usually precludes a company's hiring another underwriter and authorizes the underwriters to incur expenses in connection with the proposed offering.

LEVERAGED BUYOUT—An acquisition of an existing company using a high proportion of debt.

LIMITED OFFERING—Sales of securities exempt from registration pursuant to certain exemptions that limit the size of the offering and the number of purchasers.

MANAGING UNDERWRITERS—Also known as lead underwriters, they organize the underwriting syndicate and are the primary contact with the company.

MARKET MAKERS—The managing underwriters and some or all of the syndicated underwriters who offer to buy or sell shares at a firm price from the public, helping to sustain financial community interest and providing aftermarket support for a company's shares.

MEZZANINE FINANCING—Financial instruments that have characteristics of both debt and equity often are structured as a subordinated debt instrument with warrants to purchase an equity interest. Like venture capital, mezzanine financing generally provides the investor an opportunity to cash out the investment within several years.

NATIONAL ASSOCIATION OF SECURITIES DEALERS (NASD)—An association of U.S. securities brokers and dealers. Among other things, the NASD reviews underwriters' remuneration arrangements for all public offerings to challenge whether they are fair and reasonable.

NATIONAL ASSOCIATION OF SECURITIES DEALERS AUTOMATED QUOTATIONS (NASDAQ)—An automated information network which provides price quotations and volume information on securities traded over the counter.

OFFERING CIRCULAR—A disclosure document, similar in content to a registration statement, which is provided to investors for offerings exempt from SEC registration requirements.

OVER-THE-COUNTER MARKET—The market for securities not listed on a stock exchange.

OVERSUBSCRIBED—Refers to an IPO where the underwriter has the ability to sell more shares than it has agreed to buy from the issuer. Underwriters try to achieve this situation and as a result, exercise the overallotment option to fill those orders, resulting in additional profit for it and additional funds for the company. An oversubscribed offering will usually jump in price once the offering commences trading in the aftermarket.

PRICE-EARNINGS RATIO—The price of a share of common stock divided by earnings per share.

PRIMARY OFFERING—An offering by a company of previously unissued securities.

PRIVATE PLACEMENT—Sales of securities not involving a public offering and exempt from registration pursuant to certain exemptions.

PROSPECTUS—Part I of the registration statement, used as a selling document by the underwriting syndicate. The prospectus discloses information about the company and the offering and is distributed as a separate document or booklet to prospective investors.

PROXY—A shareholder's written authorization for some other person to represent him and vote at a shareholders' meeting.

PROXY STATEMENT—The information required by the SEC to be given to shareholders by those soliciting shareholder proxies.

PUBLIC FLOAT—The aggregate market value of the small business issuers voting stock held by nonaffiliates.

QUALIFIED INSTITUTIONAL BUYER (QIB)—A QIB is any of the following entities acting for its own account or the accounts of other QIBs, that in the aggregate owns and invests on a discretionary basis at least $100 million in securities of issuers that are not affiliated with the entity: certain insurance companies; any investment company; small business investment company; employee benefit plan; trust fund whose trustee is a bank or trust company; business development company; any organization described in 501(c)(3) of the Internal Revenue Code other than a bank or savings and loan, partnership, Massachusetts or similar business trust; and investment advisor.

RATIO OF EARNINGS TO FIXED CHARGES—An analytical tool required to be disclosed with selected financial data and in an exhibit to certain registration statements filed with the SEC. Earnings is defined as pretax income from continuing operations, plus fixed charges. Fixed charges are generally defined as total interest whether expensed or capitalized.

RED HERRING—The preliminary prospectus that is distributed to the underwriting syndicate for further distribution to prospective investors. It includes a legend in red ink on the cover stating that the registration statement has not yet become effective.

REGISTRAR AND TRANSFER AGENT—As an agent for the company, issues the securities sold to investors, maintains current records of all shareholders and their addresses, and maintains the records for subsequent transfers of securities upon resale.

REGISTRATION STATEMENT—The disclosure document filed with the SEC pursuant to the registration requirements of federal securities laws. The registration statement includes the prospectus and other information required by the SEC.

REGULATION A—SEC rules governing the exemption from registration of certain public offerings of up to $5 million.

REGULATION C—Prescribes the procedures to be followed in preparing and filing a registration statement (e.g., paper size, numbers of copies).

REGULATION D—SEC rules governing the exemptions from registration for private placements and limited offerings.

REGULATION S-B—Regulations governing financial and nonfinancial statement related disclosures in both registration statements and periodic reports filed by small business issuers.

REGULATION S-K—Regulations governing nonfinancial statement related disclosures in both registration statements and periodic reports (other than small business issuers).

REGULATION S-X—Regulations governing the form, content and periods to be covered in financial statements included in registration statements and periodic reports (other than small business issuers).

RESTRICTED STOCK—Certain shares acquired in a private placement that are subject to resale limitations.

ROAD SHOW—A series of meetings in different cities to allow members of the underwriting syndicate and prospective investors to ask company management questions relating to the company and the offering.

RULE 144—The rule governing sales of shares by controlling shareholders and holders of restricted stock.

RULE 144A—A non-exclusive safe harbor exemption from the registration requirements of the Securities Act of 1933 (1933 Act) for specified resale of restricted securities to QIBs. Securities that are eligible for resale under Rule 144A are generally initially sold by issuers in offerings which are not required to be registered under the 1933 Act.

SAFE HARBOR RULE—Commonly used to describe SEC provisions that protect issuers from possible legal actions if they have made a good faith effort to comply with certain specified requirements.

SECONDARY OFFERING—Public offerings subsequent to the IPO of previously issued shares usually held by large investors.

SECURITIES ACT OF 1933 (1933 ACT)—Generally requires that public offerings of securities be registered with the SEC before they may be sold.

SECURITIES AND EXCHANGE COMMISSION (SEC)—The government agency responsible for administration of U.S. federal securities laws, including the 1933 Act and the 1934 Act.

SECURITIES EXCHANGE ACT OF 1934 (1934 ACT)—Regulates securities exchanges and over-the-counter markets. Also, generally requires publicly held companies to file periodic reports with the SEC.

SHORT-SWING PROFITS—Profits realized by specified company insiders on transactions in the company's securities completed within a six-month period, whether or not based on insider information.

SMALL BUSINESS ISSUER—A company incorporated in the United States or Canada that has less than $25 million of revenue and public float (as defined) in the two most recent fiscal years.

STAFF ACCOUNTING BULLETINS (SABs)—SABs are published interpretations and practices followed by the staff of the SEC.

STRATEGIC PARTNERSHIP—Also known as a strategic alliance or a corporate venture, this term refers to a collaboration of a company with a larger, financially stronger company that can provide resources to meet economic and strategic goals.

TENDER OFFER—An offer, usually in an attempt to gain control of another company, to purchase existing shareholders' securities.

TOMBSTONE AD—A published notice of an offering, generally disclosing only the amount of the offering, the name of the company, a description of the security, the offering price, and the names of the underwriters.

TRANSFER AGENT—See **REGISTRAR AND TRANSFER AGENT**.

TRANSMITTAL LETTER—Used to file the registration statement with the SEC. The transmittal letter should call attention to matters of importance or uncertainty to facilitate the SEC's review of the documents. It should also confirm the results or resolutions of any informal conversations held with the SEC staff.

UNDERWRITERS—The underwriters include the managing underwriter and the underwriting syndicate. Their primary function is to purchase securities from the company and sell securities to the investing public. See also **INVESTMENT BANKERS**.

UNDERWRITING AGREEMENT—The underwriting agreement contains the details of the company's arrangements with the underwriters, including the type of underwriting (i.e., best efforts or firm commitment), the underwriters' compensation, the offering price, and number of shares.

VENTURE CAPITAL—High-risk financing, generally in the form of common stock, preferred stock convertible into common stock, or debentures convertible into common stock, often provided to companies not qualifying for other forms of financing. The venture capital investor requires a potential for exceptionally high returns and will structure the investment so that it can be liquidated through an initial public offering or otherwise, generally within three to seven years.

INDEX